CONFESSIONS

OF AN

ENTREPRENEUR

LIVING WITH FEAR AND CHANGE
IN LIFE AND SMALL BUSINESS

Orrin,

Continue to inspire !

Annie Richard

Ann-Marie Richard

The opinions expressed in this manuscript are solely the opinions of this author.

Confessions of an Entrepreneur: Living with Fear and Change in Life and Small Business

Dedication

This book is dedicated to
George Richard
My husband provided endless encouragement to write this book.
He endured my "highs and lows" and never abandoned me when my fear of failure and
belief in myself overwhelmed me.

Anthony Pietrovito *(Deceased)*
My dad who taught me to never stop believing in myself.
Dad, if you can hear me, I promise to appreciate life for the journey it offers,
to live life with integrity and purpose, and to share life with others based upon
mutual trust and respect.

Acknowledgements

I gratefully acknowledge the guidance, love and support from my family and friends: My husband, George; Mom and Dad, who never left me wanting; My amazing daughter, Erin who by far is my greatest gift of life; brother James and sister-in-law Janet, the most caring people I know; Cousins Marie and Rosalind, friends first, family always. Sandy Strauss, Faye Fulton and Paula Lesso encouraged me to tell my story and not worry about whether anyone would want to read it or not— Just because! Thank you for that support.

So many people influenced my professional life. Gurus such as Stephen Covey, Michael Gerber, Jim Collin, John Maxwell, Jack Canfield, Orrin Woodward, Chris Brady, Tony Robbins, and Seth Godin are just a tip of my iceberg. I've read and re-read their books over the years and they provide me with new insights each time.

Business and life coach Jeff Burrows opened my eyes to realizing I was the one getting in the way of my desired outcomes. Jeff changed my way of thinking about business and life and how the two forces are inseparable. There were other Safeguard™ Distributors that were a part of the Jeff Burrows' *Entrepreneurs' Success Code*™ participants: Karen Price (deceased), Ted Mabry, Marty Pomerantz and Mike Sowers who shared their ideas, insights and genuine friendship in so many ways. Their influence was the catalyst for me being where I am today. My friends from the Safeguard™ Corporate world offered me guidance, management training and friendship.

To my editor, Glenn Proctor, thank you for your encouragement and relentless drive to get me to sit down and write this book. To editor, Dr. James Pietrovito— thank you for your suggestions and sharing your insights and knowledge of our family history.

And finally, all those special people who bought into my business dreams and helped make them a reality: Bruce Whitbeck (employee, confidante and friend), John Wheeler (now deceased, founder and original owner of the SkiRack, Burlington, VT), Joyce Zorn (now deceased, Business Development Manager for Safeguard™). There are so many, many more people who have altered my world, allowed me to wonder and helped me "growing-up." Thank you.

Table of Contents

.

Preface

"In another moment down went Alice after
it never once considering how in the world
she was to get out again."

-Lewis Carroll, <u>Alice's Adventures in Wonderland</u>

Lewis Carroll's tales, <u>Alice's Adventures in Wonderland</u> and <u>Through the Looking Glass and What Alice Found There</u>[1] present perfect allegories to modern-day people struggling for recognition, growth and survival in an ever-changing, unpredictable business environment.

There are so many business experts who espouse to have discovered the miracle for entrepreneurial success. Too often, these self-help gurus are no different than the snake-oil peddlers who traveled around small-town America through the 1800s[2]. Their false claims for miracle cures often are based upon a prior corporate job experience that earned them their "six-figure income" and a sugar-coated presentation that draws-in naïve entrepreneurs desperately in need of direction through the chaotic world of business. Many have never owned or managed a business of their own.

If you are looking for a new revelation in these pages, you will be disappointed. It is not here. What you will find is a condensed version of one woman's plunge into "business-land" and the life-altering perceptions she experienced along the way. This is about me. It is my catharsis of 30 years creating and recreating my reality of entrepreneurship. Although this is something women starting out in business can relate to, it is not intended to be biased to gender. No matter how people minimize the ups and downs of owning one's business, the greatest challenge to me is the never-ending journey to self-discovery. At each juncture along the way, I had to find happiness within myself and appreciate having experienced and survived both my mistakes and successes. These experiences I wish to share with you.

I use the "Alice in Wonderland" stories to provide playful imagery to serious undertaking. Living the life of an entrepreneur is no easy feat. A little levity keeps me from taking myself too seriously. I find it fascinating that the two children's stories written by mathematician Charles Lutwidge Dodgson (pen-name, Lewis Carroll) in the late 1800s continue to appeal after 200 years. His stories have been enjoyed by all ages and have been the basis for poems and plays, politics and satire, movies, songs and creative works of art.

No one can definitively label the character of Alice as one type of personality. That is what makes it so easy for me to appreciate her. She represents both the hopes and fears in me as I struggle to find out who I am and how I fit in this world I have created.

In Wonderland, the possibilities are endless. Alice's adventures are amplified by her growing and shrinking into different sizes. This instability of personal identity and lack of vision troubles Alice but she manages somehow to push-on despite all her shortcomings. Even the pointless and fickle behaviors of the Wonderland creatures reveal an underlying story perfectly adaptable to the entrepreneur experience where fiction and reality often collide.

As a business professional, can I recapture what the world looks like through a child's eyes? Can I let go once and for all those deceptions of what I think a successful business *should* be and focus instead on what a successful business *can* be? I certainly will give it a try!

Thinking back, my decision to give up teaching and go into business was much like Alice chasing after a white rabbit who talks to himself. I was frustrated and unhappy with the limitations imposed within the brick and mortar of a public high school in a small town. My personal life was hanging by a thread. I was looking for a 'way out' or a 'way-in'— someplace where I felt I was in control.

Why not start my own business?

I will be my own boss! I will call the shots!

I might even be rich some day!

I will create a legacy to be proud of!

This would be my destiny!

And so, I jumped…

down that rabbit hole…

It was a long way down…

and dark.

SEEK and HIDE

*Alice: "Would you tell me, please, which way I ought
to go from here?'
"That depends a good deal on where you want to get to,'
said the Cat.
`I don't much care where--' said Alice.
'Then it doesn't matter which way you go,' said the Cat.
--so long as I get SOMEWHERE,' Alice added
as an explanation.
Oh, you're sure to do that,' said the Cat, `if you only
walk long enough."*

-*Lewis Carroll, Alice's Adventures in Wonderland*

I could tell you that I followed some great vision that
came to me in a dream. I could tell you I became an
entrepreneur and despite all odds, defied insurmountable
obstacles and emerged into entrepreneurial glory of great
wisdom, wealth and pure, unadulterated joy. But that would be
far from the truth.

Just like Alice, I saw my life as more of the same familiar
expectations and routines with limitations. I jumped at the
opportunity to follow that elusive rabbit into unknown territory.
My need to take things beyond face value would prove to be
both a weakness and a gift: unfolding a succession of endless
wandering through-the-weeds of ideas only to delight in a
treasure-trove of discovery by maintaining certain ideals that
would keep me on firm ground.

Truth is, I didn't have an inkling of what I was getting
myself into. If I had, would I have stuck to teaching high

school English Lit and Theatre Arts? Perhaps, for a few more years. For six years, I mainly taught English electives for grades 9 through 12 and managed and directed the drama program. It was difficult for me to follow the prescribed curriculum. I struggled with the opinion that if what I was assigned to teach couldn't hold *my* attention, why should I expect it to hold my students' attention? It just seemed wrong. I needed to find a way to inspire them to want to learn.

The study of grammar and punctuation never seemed a chore to me. Even when attending elementary school, part of understanding correct grammar was learning how to diagram sentences. It was like putting a puzzle together, and I loved that there is a reason why certain words fit together into a sentence. I have gained an appreciation for good writing through lots of practice reading it and my attempts to write.

When I taught these subjects, I tossed in an extra study of the evolution of the English language. How miraculous is the power of our written and spoken words! Language is arbitrary and takes on the environment around it. Lewis Carroll's stories are most entertaining with his comical take on school and the use of words to effectively communicate.

From when I was a child, my favorite alone-time was reading. My dad purchased a set of encyclopedias for my brother and me. Along with it came 10 volumes of assorted short stories, a collection of Grimm's fairy tales and other classics. I read them all, cover-to-cover, many times over. My passion for reading has continued throughout my life: classics, sci-fi, biographies, fantasy, murder and mystery. It was natural for me to turn to self-help, business, sales, marketing and other professional books as an entrepreneur. Books have been my escape and my refuge. They have provided a source of new ideas, inspirations and fantasies.

Being in business for myself is often a lonely space so I depend on the expertise and perspectives of other people who have experienced what it takes to survive and flourish in 'Business-land'.

"'When I use a word,' Humpty Dumpty said in rather a scornful tone, 'it means just what I choose it to mean —neither more nor less.'
'The question is,' said Alice, 'whether you can make words mean so many different things.'
'The question is,' said Humpty Dumpty, 'which is to be master — that's all.'"
  -Lewis Carroll, Alice's Adventures in Wonderland

Think about the importance of the 20 to 30-second 'elevator speech' business professionals use to introduce themselves. I can't tell you the number of times I have written and re-written my introduction. I know for certain, it will continue to evolve to meet my needs:

- Utilize words that will express my vision through the brief, succinct description that sets me apart from my competition

- Adapt my introduction using different descriptive words, phrases or examples to avoid monotony and maintain my audience's attention

- Draft my introduction with words that consider who the audience is and what appeals to their needs

- Deliver my introduction with genuine vitality and heartfelt belief

- Make direct eye contact with as many people who are listening

- Frequently rehearse my introduction to remind me of my goals and reinforce a proper mindset

Along with boredom for my high school's standardized curriculum, I felt undervalued and under-paid for my efforts, and uncomfortably restricted by the bureaucracies of the public-school system. Rather than accepting the system and the certainty of my ability and courage to question it openly, I chose to change direction and follow another life path. I trusted that self-employment was the answer, was eager to accept the challenge and widely curious. Could this business idea work?

Stephen H. Covey in his book <u>The 8th Habit</u>, talks about how our ability to change our habits will require knowledge, attitude and skill coming together to take on new challenges and open the door to limitless possibilities[1]. Alice first discovers this notion in Wonderland and eventually comes to believe it for herself:

"*Alice laughed. 'There's no use trying,' she said. 'One can't believe impossible things.'*

'I daresay you haven't had much practice,' said the Queen. 'When I was your age, I always did it for half-an-hour a day.' 'Why, sometimes I've believed as many as six impossible things before breakfast.' (The Queen)

- Lewis Carroll, *Alice's Adventures in Wonderland*

The Idea: *Annie's Honor Snacks* is conceived.

I remember clearly the day I was introduced to a business idea for a snack service. It took hold of me and wouldn't let go. The snack service was an uncle's brainstorm after he met someone who had launched a similar business in an affluent suburb outside of Philadelphia.

Not only did this uncle provide the idea for the business, he offered me an added enticement that was difficult to abandon. He and Dad had formed a business partnership and their company would provide the necessary financing to get the business up and running. My role was to manage operations and control the marketing efforts. I couldn't possibly go wrong. And so, the concept of *Annie's Honor Snacks* was born.

The day I handed the superintendent of schools my letter of resignation was momentous. I went home and called my uncle. "Okay, I'm ready to get started," I said, enthusiastically. "I am committed to doing this." His reply was, "Great. Let me talk to your dad and we'll get back to you."

And then I waited.

My uncle and Dad called me back three days later. They

had been talking. When the conversation began with, 'Don't quit your teaching job yet,' I got a sick feeling in my stomach. You see, they had come up with a special condition. They would only support this endeavor if my husband (of my first marriage) had nothing to do with it.

Husband #1 and my Italian-American family were often at odds with each other and I found myself caught in-the-middle. I was taught that respect, responsibility and duty to the family came first and hard work was a close second. He had difficulty accepting standards that fell outside his comfort zone. My family also saw things I blindly refused to see. I chose to pass off his excessive drinking, substance abuse and mood swings as minor occurrences. I convinced myself to believe that he could control these indulgences.

My parents were first generation Americans and had assimilated into middle-class America. Where their parents occasionally spoke the mother tongue, my parents did not. They were accepting of most individuals, even those whose values differed from their own but (to quote my brother), with a lot of red sauce and garlic! We were a traditional Italian-American family, to the letter.

Meal-time was a time to nourish both the body and the soul. Everyone was expected to join in the conversation, eat everything on their plate and stay seated until everyone was through eating. Holiday dining could last hours, with many conversations and emotions going at once.

My uncle and my father's conditional support for the business collided with my determination to be loyal to my spouse. This was painful for me and in some ways a relief. Their true feelings about my marriage were finally out in the open. It became my personal motivator to make certain I would succeed. I'd already quit my respectable, secure teaching position to launch this business.

That was my first mistake in becoming an entrepreneur. Now I was without a salary, benefits and guaranteed time-off. I wasn't prepared for going it alone especially knowing that my dependency on my spouse was shaky at best. I had a business plan that left too much to chance and a budget that was negligible for what I was proposing to accomplish.

The truly crazy part was that no one challenged my decision to move forward with the business venture for the right reasons. I got away with it because I was a woman and shouldn't need to be a major "bread-winner" of the family. They thought it would become a passing fancy. I would eventually tire of this business and return to teaching.

My parents would have been relieved if I would have chosen to be a stay-at-home mom, raising my children, doing the household chores and having a hot dinner ready for the table when my husband came home. After all, this was a good life for my mom, why shouldn't it be good enough for me? I was wanting so much more: adventure and freedom to pursue the unexpected and develop my own place in the world.

The love between my parents and myself has always been unwavering. We never allow differences to come between us. But, in a family dominated by strong males, I always lingered in the background. Expectations for a woman in my family had never been equal to those of a man. Things that I felt passionate about often were dismissed or devalued in some way. I resented that terribly but often allowed negativity and self-doubt to rule me.

Whereas I might have felt left-out, I've no doubt my brother had the constant pressure to excel. My big brother has often been my compass at times when I've felt most afraid to venture forth on my own. I followed in his footsteps since we were children walking to elementary school. I followed his path to college in Williamsport, Pennsylvania, and within a year after I graduated from college, I traced his steps once again and began a new life in Vermont. My insecurities often made me more afraid of my possible successes than I was of my failures.

My 50s upbringing with "Father Knows Best"[2] and "Leave It to Beaver"[3] exemplified the ideal life that my parents wished for me. "I Love Lucy"[4] and "The Honeymooners"[5] were fascinating to me. The women could be adventurous and silly and the men weren't always right just because they were men. Ralph (Jackie Gleason) could frighten me with his temper, but then amaze me with his vulnerability. As a teenager, Mary Tyler Moore[6] showed that a woman can compete with men in the business world and thrive.

There is no hurt quite like the pain or frustration I have experienced when I've felt powerless and misunderstood by family members or friends. I relive these and other memories of past experiences, reconstructing the conversations into wishful outcomes that might have been. It has shaped me and influenced my ability to interact with others I meet. If I discipline myself before I react to something without thought, I only set myself up to continue to disappoint and be disappointed. Whatever seems impossible at the time may just be a matter of my limited point of view.

My greatest regret is that I didn't get to really know my dad as a person until many years later when my first marriage collapsed and I became a single parent with a business to run. A week never went by without the two of us talking, sometimes for hours, on the phone. He was my confidant and friend. He was an honorable man and was often underestimated by the people closest to him. Dad passed way in 2000. I miss him every day of my life.

Mom now lives with George (we married in 1994) and me. She is still going strong at 90 years old, baking cookies, making home-made lasagna and meatballs, and fussing about the house. I'm fortunate to still have her. To this day, I don't think she comprehends what I do for business, but that's okay. She teaches me to be grateful each day and that it is my source of true potential.

The Vision: *Annie's Honor Snacks* is born.

This business venture I was determined to make happen was uncharted territory. I knew so very little about starting a business including not knowing what questions to even ask. Google didn't exist. I still had resources available through agencies such as the Small Business Administration. The library and book stores had racks of self-help books. But there was nothing to prepare me for the day-in-day-out stresses

I would have to face as a business owner and the deep feelings of isolation.

I absorbed what information I could and created a business plan.   This was wise. I was heading in the right direction by creating my road map. The business plan may have looked good on paper and met the guidelines recommended in books, but it only worked in theory. I discovered it needed strategies incorporated into it for putting the plan into action.

Another concern I found with subsequent business plans, was for all they were worth, they lacked humanity. The special ingredients of honor, service and commitment combined with a workable plan would produce loyal employees, life-time customers and future legacies. My family was the first to teach me these life-lessons but it was up to me to put them to use in my business.

My entrepreneurial traits have frequently shared the characteristics of the introverted extrovert: not exactly comfortable in my own clothing, but no longer willing to put on the outfit someone else selected for me to wear. Since I created the ideas born from dreams, frustrations or visions of a different world-- no matter the underlying cause, they always were dependent on a need for change. Every day, I could choose to wake up a different person with new thoughts and ideas to find and put into practice.

Annie's Honor Snacks was a concept I tweaked with my personal traits and morphed into my own customized, home-based snack and catering service. It was a simple, sole-proprietorship that experienced the same demands and required forethought that any business large or small, requires.

I fell in love with the belief that I could provide other businesses with an employee benefit at no direct expense to the participating company. Furthermore, I could ascertain that it would increase employee morale, trust, and productivity. Considerably less obtrusive than a vending machine and with no service fee, employees could enjoy their entire scheduled breaks without having to leave the premises and drive or walk someplace to buy something to eat or drink. I knew if I made my business necessary, I would always be needed.

Why was it called 'honor-snacks?' The service was based upon the honor system of payment. I provided the initial dollars' worth of change in an attached plastic container. I encouraged people to make their own change as needed. All I asked, "Just pay for whatever you take out of the snack box." If people didn't pay, they would risk losing the service.

When what I feel is meaningfully expressed in my business, it attracts others to want to engage in a relationship with me. I first must develop an ability to identify my own emotions. A term for this is emotional intelligence. I probably can't change my IQ or my personality but with dedicated practice I can positively change my EQ. According to Travis Bradberry and Jean Greaves in their book Emotional Intelligence 2.0, EQ accounts for 58 percent of performance no matter what type of job or IQ level and is the foundation for a host of critical skills such as leadership and personal excellence[7]. I become what I believe I am.

Through *Annie's Honor Snacks,* I built a company whose entire existence depended upon trusting relationships. Trust must be mutual if it can truly exist. To this day, I still want to believe that most people are willing to pay for convenience and quality and will do so when they get what they want.

I cannot emphasize enough how much *Annie's Honor Snacks'* success was linked to the ethical responsibility of people to be honest and trustworthy. If a change box was shorted on the prior visit, we would place a small yellow adhesive note to the box with the missing amount written on it as a reminder. I faithfully tracked our shortage rate on a weekly basis. Ninety-four percent of the time, the shortage was made up.

There were many instances where people over-paid because they knew the box was 'short-changed" the week before, either by themselves or covering for someone else. One day, on a Monday morning service route, I picked up the box and found a sealed envelope with my name written on it. The note inside read: *"Dear Annie, please accept this $25 towards our snack box. I had to work over the weekend and didn't have a sitter for my two kids. They found the snack box and raided it. My fault we ran out of snacks sooner than planned. I'm so sorry! I hope this covers it."*

Small professional businesses employing under 25 people were eighty percent of my accounts. Included in that group were bank branches. One such branch was so small it did not have a break room for its employees. The solution: they kept the snack box in the bank's vault. When I would deliver them a snack box with freshly replenished products, they would "buzz" me in and give me access into the vault!

The Focus: *Annie's Honor Snacks learns about perseverance.*

Could an *Annie's Honor Snacks* concept survive and thrive in today's marketplace? I'm not sure. As a society, it seems imperative to secure our defenses and limit exposing our vulnerability. Hope is eternal and I choose to believe it resides at the core of the entrepreneurial spirit in each of us.

Whenever I pursue a new business venture spurred-on by my restlessness and discontent with the way things are, I am reminded in short time that I am being delusional if I expect those feelings to disappear. In part, they are my incentive to act. It is the difference between acts of impulsiveness and a clear vision for making it real that justifies its importance.

Alice is just as frustrated and unhappy with her life in Wonderland as she is in her real world because she has no purpose or vision to follow. She is too preoccupied with following others and adapting to their style. At one point in the story, Alice completely forgets who she is. It is okay not to have all the answers or even knowing the right road to travel down. There's always a lesson to be learned. What is critical is understanding why I'm doing it in the first place.

A significant part of my professional life has been working with other entrepreneurs. I've found that belief in their dream is never lacking. They love the work and they are fulfilling a need they see in themselves. They envision helping others to be fulfilled as well. What they often can't see is the difference between being a hobbyist and being a business owner. The hobbyist can afford to indulge in the timeless joy of the activity but the entrepreneur must see the activity through a new perspective of time and monetary investments resulting in profitability.

Chris Brady and Orrin Woodward in their book, Financial Fitness, discuss how most people never achieve their life dreams because they get distracted by financial fads and get rich quick schemes. To make matters worse, there's the massive influence from big companies with huge advertising and marketing budgets that convince us that we must have what they are selling.[8] Alice decides at the end of the first book, that the creatures of Wonderland are nothing more than a pack of cards. Since it is her dream, she will decide what is real.

Once my vision is realized, there are three fundamental absolutes that all my business endeavors must have: financial stability, management standards and strategic marketing. Relying on skills, talents and brains just aren't enough to build a successful business in today's constantly changing and competitive environment. By reinforcing these pillars with persistence, determination and hard work, I have a fighting chance to achieve my goals. I have learned this the hard way and I'd be lying to you if I said I have this mastered today. The difference is my mindset. It allows me to recognize what needs fixing.

My 30-plus years of entrepreneurship have convinced me that only when these three elements sync with each other will my business bring me the joy and success that I envision. I've launched several business ventures over the years, but that first endeavor, *Annie's Honor Snacks*, in the early 1980s in Vermont, completed my metamorphosis from employee to employer. This first venture was like stepping through the looking-glass above the fireplace in Alice's family drawing-room. I got my first glimpse of living a dream of my own making. What a rush!

"ALICE
She drank from a bottle called DRINK ME
And she grew so tall,
She ate from a plate called TASTE ME
And down she shrank so small.
And so she changed, while other folks
Never tried nothin' at all."
> (Shel Silverstein, Where the Sidewalk Ends:
> The Poems and Drawings of Shel Silverstein") [9]

Always On My Toes

With each new venture, the necessities for financial stability and management standards reminded me that I still had a lot to learn. This was work. Whether physically entrenched in the operations of the business or providing the leadership for others to get the job done, I frequently had to do a self-assessment to know if I was up for it. I had to rely on my resiliency to keep scratching at the bite until I could relieve its itch with a resolve that would carry me through. The solution often wasn't readily apparent. Sometimes I mistook what I thought was the problem to be something else entirely. I was taught to learn from past mistakes, but unfortunately, that usually meant I had to first survive them.

> "I wish I hadn't cried so much!" said Alice, as she swam about, trying to find her way out.
> "I shall be punished for it now, I suppose, by drowning in my own tears.
>
> -Lewis Carroll, *Alice's Adventures in Wonderland*

In the first two years of *Annie's Honor Snacks*, our inventory was always lean because of our extremely tight budget. There were two disasters that nearly wiped us out. An unusual abundance of winter snow storms, rain, and early spring thaw, caused an unusual amount of flooding throughout the state and severely damaged inventory stored in our basement. We had lived in that home for four years and never experienced any unwanted moisture or water.

This major set-back caused us to rethink our existing operating system, how we preserved and recycled inventory, and our process for packing boxes. Our homeowner's insurance deductible was set high to keep our monthly premium cost down and wouldn't be enough to help us with the replacement cost. Upon further inquiries, it was questionable whether we could even have a claim since it was a business loss. We had never considered the need to adjust our insurance policy coverage.

Our solution was to convert our garage into a warehouse, parking in the driveway or alongside the house. We had to consider that on-street parking was banned in Vermont during the winter months to allow snow plows to get through. Moving to the garage seemed like a great solution. We gained a waterproof staging and storage area. It was a minimal expense to cover the cost of shelving, insulation and a kerosene heater. Unloading and loading the snack boxes into the vans was more easily accomplished. Certainly, it saved some wear and tear on our house.

Three days before Christmas 1982, disaster struck again. The kerosene heater in the garage malfunctioned during the night and started a fire. We saved the building (and our home) but smoke and water damage completely wiped out most of our inventory and nearly closed us down. The temperatures were in the single digits and our juices had frozen. Broken glass, black and greasy soot covered everything. All snack boxes had to be soaked in hot water, scrubbed and disinfected—a huge undertaking.

It was 4 am in the morning. I remember my three-month-old daughter crying to be nursed. We were exhausted. My husband sat on the couch with his head in his hands, saying: "This is it. We are done. There's no way we can come back from this disaster."

I called my employee, and an hour later she was at our door. I fed my baby, gave her a kiss and tucked her into her crib as she began to doze. I looked at my husband and said, "Get up. This is not over yet. We must find a way because this business is not just about us. Other people are depending on us. Besides, there is no other option but to keep going."

We all went to work.

I know that how I treated these lows and highs in my life defined me. Those events are forever etched in my memories. But it was the little things, the day-to-day activities, that time I invested in routines that made the difference in my successes. They often seemed mundane and insignificant yet when executed with purpose, they kept me from merely being a victim to chance or circumstance. They provided me the room to make choices not only when the time was right but also when the unexpected occurred. Michael Gerber, small business consultant and author of The E-Myth, talks about how having a process in place for developing a business becomes a way of going to work on our lives and not just our way of doing things.[1]

I realize that most entrepreneurs will not reach the monetary heights of the Bill Gates, Oprah Winfrey, Mark Zuckerberg or Cher Wang of this world, and that includes me. But each time I overcome the obstacles that get in my way, I move closer to achieving what matters the most in my life: a desire to be better and do better in business and in relationships. When I give myself fully to something, I am injecting my energy and spirit into it until I can rightfully own it. That is why I believe business and life should serve each other rather than exist on opposing sides, straining for attention.

A professional colleague, Marty Pomerantz, came up with an acronym for the word A.W.A.R.E.™: Acknowledge What Activities Result in Excellence. I believe it belongs right up there with the Golden Rule, "Do to others as you would have them do to you." Know your destination, set your headings carefully and always use your compass to stay on track. Then unfurl the sails, untangle those lines, and let her go!

Alice's journey in Through the Looking Glass followed the moves of a chess game. Anyone who has ever participated or observed a serious game of chess, knows that successful players are always alert and in full control of their anticipated moves. But Alice entered Wonderland through a looking glass, so everything was in reverse—getting where she wanted to go meant walking in the opposite direction or she'd continuously find herself back at the beginning. She kept trying until she finally could move forward.

In the story, even the country-side is based on a game of chess with its grassy fields and valleys patterned into squares. Most main characters are represented by a chess piece or an animal, with Alice herself being a pawn. She is promised by the

Queen that when she reaches the eighth square, she will become a queen. That is Alice's objective. Typical of Wonderland, Alice's journey is a mishmash of confusion, detours and wishful thinking.

The pawn is the chess piece of lowest value. It moves one square at a time and is manipulated to further the player's win. I have allowed myself to be a pawn when I didn't stay alert to all the variables that could impact me. Other times I chose this role because I elected to only move forward one small step at a time while I carefully kept my eye on the goal. But sometimes, with the unpredictability of life, my business presented situations I did not perceive. The more risks I took, the more likely the odds that I would experience failure.

Failure need not be an end but an integral part of the growth process. Where my good experiences and joyful occasions have become cherished memories, it is the difficulties, hardships and misfortunes—call them what you will— that evolve into lessons learned. I can't control the world, but I can impact it for the better if I am determined to be a productive and attentive occupant.

I've always had two basic ways of dealing with life: either I took ownership of my thoughts, feelings and opinions and turned them into actions or I caved-in and became a victim. It always has come down to these two choices. When I have chosen the first way, the entrepreneurial mindset, I reinvented myself. I expand my outward thinking with a compassion, vision and courage to move in a forward direction. When I allowed myself to be the victim, I shrunk within myself and became isolated from others and crippled.

A good day for me is when I begin it with anticipation of what I pre-planned for the day to unfold. I adjust the demands of my business to better reflect my goals and chosen lifestyle. I rarely have two days the same with a fluctuating work schedule and I love that. What I accomplish each day should fit within the operational parameters of my business. It depends on following standardized systematic processes that kept me on track and at task.

My goal is to ensure that my personal and professional life reside in comfortable proximity to each other. Whether it is managing my family routines, supervising employees, project development work or facilitating a seminar for a group of professionals, a systematic approach grounds me and gives me the stability and continuity needed to function effectively. The most logical way to achieve this consistently is to develop written systems so these tasks can be repeated and refreshed as needed. I call this my Operations Manual. This is when the manager in me must come to the forefront and take charge.

Annie's Honor Snacks had lots of systems for its operations. Despite our planning, I often had to change them or replace them altogether. Initially, most of these processes were reactive to an immediate need. As I gained experience, I learned to be proactive by anticipating the needs and developing systems that would manage them. Here are some examples we used:

- Customized Snack Menu: Our product lines were constantly changing as vendors adjusted their product lines and customers' tastes varied. I produced a new updated menu seasonally, allowing me to publicize product offerings and attract new interest. It took on the characteristics of a newsletter when I shared an event or special recognition of my honor snack customers. If I was going to offer options, I'd better be sure to have the inventory readily available to cover those selections or not offer them in the first place.

- Inventory control: All our products had expiration dates and most were not returnable. Like a grocery store, we had to rotate inventory, restock and only distribute those items that had not expired or were damaged. We had to remove products whose expiration date would happen before the next scheduled date for servicing.

- Production Line: We utilized a system for filling the snack boxes and loading delivery vehicles. At first, we refilled the boxes at the business's site, and found it too time consuming having to go back and forth from the van. We also couldn't anticipate what items would be required since contents were based on the customers' eating habits that week. Our solution was to fill the boxes back at the house, then stack them in order of the delivery route. The used boxes were swapped-out and replaced with a new, freshly packed box.

- Scheduled delivery routes: The size of company, location and accessibility were determining factors for assigning them to a driver and mapping out the specific route to follow.

  - Each day's scheduled routes consisted of a combination of weekly, twice-a-week and three-times-a-week visits. We were on a first name basis with nearly all our customers and they depended on us showing up on their scheduled servicing day.

- Box identity: Each customer was assigned an account number that was printed upon two interchangeable change boxes. This facilitated the tallying of snack returns and crediting money received to the correct account. Inventory and money received was counted back at the house.

- A computer program: I tracked the eating habits of my customers and calculated whether the money deposited in the coin box corresponded to what was consumed. A local programmer developed a customized system to do this. (In case you are wondering, and despite the noble pleading for healthy snacks, Snickers™ candy bars were by far the most popular treat).

- Survey: We found customer feedback invaluable. Their input led me to expand the product lines to include lunch catering and coffee services. They were happy and so was I. The more they depended on me, the more likely I would retain that customer relationship.

- Public service: I found it difficult to find funds or personnel to contribute to the many non-profit organizations in our community. We looked at leftover or soon-to-be expired inventory and we donated it to the local food shelf every Friday. Perhaps it wasn't very nutritious, but the occasional coffee cake and cup of hot cocoa or coffee was considered a valued gift.

The methodology for system development followed me into my next enterprise as an independent distributor for *Safeguard Business Systems, Inc.*™, a long-established print manufacturer. Its signature product, the One-Write™ check writing system provided one-step bookkeeping systems for small businesses and revolutionized the bookkeeping industry before affordable computerization came on the scene.

My company was called *AERIN, Inc.*, named after my daughter and me. I started out with close to 450 active business accounts. These accounts combined with the relationships I had developed through *Annie's Honor Snacks* gave me great access to the small business community. I was actively involved in the Vermont Chamber of Commerce, Vermont Home Builders & Remodelers Association and

Women's Business Owners Network, to name a few. I frequently had opportunities to participate in professional speaking engagements. When I sold the business in 2010, I had more than four thousand active customers ordering annually. With employees and independent sales reps working for me in two different states, my operations manual was the one consistently reliable connection we had with one another. I needed to know that everyone was working together to achieve the same goals. Even the simple routine of opening the office in the morning, checking for messages, turning on computers and retrieving the prior night's backup tapes from our mainframe computer needed to be translated into a standardized system that anyone could follow. Everyone in my organization had direct access to the operations manual and was responsible for learning and contributing to those systems that directly related to their position on my team.

I learned that a business without defined systems to support it, is like a sand castle on the beach before the tide comes in. It just won't endure. Its demise may be slow and hardly noticeable at first. At some point, it will collapse, quickly wash away and soon be forgotten. In an unpredictable world, I need to manage with intent and stack the odds in my favor.

Although I function best when I have rules and structure to guide me, I question those rules as my needs evolve. If I follow them blindly I risk becoming complacent. That is why operation manuals and other such tools should be updated at least once a year, and reviewed every six months. These plans are not designed to have the permanence of stone tablets. If I am too set in my ways, I may miss opportunities ready for the taking or incur unwarranted problems. It is much too easy to get mired with things that are beyond my control.

I certainly experienced this with *Annie's Honor Snacks* and it didn't stop there. With each subsequent business venture, I anguished over the things I couldn't control instead of focusing on why they happened in the first place.

> *"Always speak the truth, think before you speak, and write it down afterwards."*
>
> -Lewis Carroll, *Alice's Adventures in Wonderland*

WHEN Duty Calls

We have all become a cynical lot. The constant change in the ways we communicate can be frightening and tumultuous. With the wondrous freedom and convenience that modern technology has brought us, many have sought comfort in isolating themselves behind computer screens and cell phones. Ironically, it has left us vulnerable to hackers, identity thieves and other exploiters.

It has become more and more difficult to separate truth from reality. News may or may not be believed. Vulgarity and slanderous tweets are commonplace. Fundamental beliefs and traditions have been shaken to the core. Our schools prepare our children for jobs that will no longer exist when they graduate. The ideals of American democracy as inscribed on our Statue of Liberty: "Give me your tired, your poor, your huddled masses yearning to breathe free" –those ideals once symbolic of hope for a better life, now are shrouded in doubt or fear.

My Accountability to Me

I must bear the responsibility for not only my life, but my impact on others. I hate the phrase, 'It's nothing personal… just business.' Of course, it is personal! Everything is personal or should be. A business owner must constantly be diligent to understand and honestly relate to customers' needs and desires. At the same time, consideration of the challenges employees face both at work and at home should never be denied or ignored. I can no more leave my personal life outside the office door and then expect employees to miraculously do the impossible. However, I can learn ways to better cope and offer solutions to others when possible.

Without getting too philosophical, I have only one life to live. It is solely my responsibility to take good care of my body, mind and spirit. I can stimulate my thoughts by using the myriad of educational resources available to help keep my mind alert and attentive to the changes around me. As for my body, I can't stop time from aging it, but I can certainly delay its effects.

According to the U.S. Census Bureau, I am a member of the baby boomer generation—those individuals born between mid-1946 and mid-1964. Projections of the entire older population (which includes the pre-baby boomer, those born prior to 1946) suggests that 71.4 million people will be age 65 or older in 2029.[1] That same report predicts that by 2035, the difference between old age dependency and youth dependency will be less than two percent.

I am acutely aware that if I don't start taking better care of myself I am in for a world of hurt. The good news is life expectancy has increased significantly over the past fifty years. The bad news for some of us is that we haven't paid better attention to what we put into our bodies, how we have allowed stress to be our daily companion and despite the 401K and other investments, many people I know remain in debt.

It is not surprising that there is a growing demand for wellness products, particularly in the organic personal care and beauty products. Grand View Research issued a report stating that this industry is expected to reach an unprecedented $16 billion by 2020[2]. The following figures show the increases beginning in 2010:

- Pilates and yoga studios: 2.8 percent, $7 billion in revenue, 113,000 workers
- Gyms, health and fitness clubs: 2.2 percent, $30 billion in revenue, 702,000 workers
- Health and wellness spas: 2.7 percent, $16 billion in revenue, 359,000 workers

For as long as I can remember, my personal albatross has been my weight. I've yo-yoed over the years, from the numerous diets and fads—always vowing that this time, I'm going to lose the weight for good. I have a closet filled with clothes of different sizes to adapt to my body's ever-changing expansion and contraction. Here's just a few of my litany of excuses:

- I have a crazy schedule and don't have time to plan meals, let alone prepare them

- Mom tempts me with her delicious deserts and home-cooking

- I eat out at least 4 meals per week attending work related activities

- I tire of boring diet food; and it embarrasses me to draw attention to myself to order it in public

- I'm just too tired to exercise

- I've got too much work to do in the office to take an hour off to go for a walk

- And on, and on ....

Now look what I've done! I have just confessed my personal lack of self-discipline to the world in this book! This is the time for me to face my self-defeating monster once and for all. As the Duchess liked to tell Alice:

> *"Tut, tut, child! Everything's got a moral, if only you can find it."*
>
> *- Lewis Carroll, Alice's Adventures in Wonderland*

How I respect and care for myself carries a lasting impression on the attitude others will direct towards me as I set the stage for business relationships. My life experiences with family and close friends has greatly influenced my attitude and my behavior. I might choose to deceive myself and hide behind a false image that I present to strangers, but it is rare that my family cannot see through my façade. They know me in so very many ways.

It is a relief when I permit myself to let down the barriers, relax and just be me with others. Lessons learned through family relationships have taught me to accept that differences make each person uniquely special. Wouldn't it be grand if everyone could feel safe enough to always be their authentic self? Disciplined and responsible living habits should naturally influence professional habits.

Family Accountability

The generations that preceded me are a part of my psyche. I also have had to unlearn certain biases, programing and limited world-view that was a part of the culture that groomed me. My grandparents on both sides of the family were Italian immigrants who came to this country with the hopes for a better and more prosperous life than would befall them if they stayed in the old country. They were adventurous and clever with very little formal education.

My dad experienced the loneliness of being an only child growing up as his only sibling was born 20 years later. He turned to his extended family of first and second cousins and friends to fill the need for joy and companionship in his life. I remember my grandmother (Nana) as a reserved woman who rarely showed open signs of affection. She was devoutly Catholic yet still adhered to old Italian traditions and folklore.

My place in the family was to keep out of trouble, act 'like a lady' and be 'seen and not heard.' I was to stay with the women and help in the kitchen. There was no allowance for me to be included in any boy activities such as playing catch or climbing trees.

My fraternal grandparents had an arranged marriage. My grandfather (Nano) was much older than his young teenage bride. Nano worked for the railroad but his vocation was gardening. It was a time when putting money into property paid off. He worked hard and invested in three property lots adjacent to the land the family home was built on. From this he created an immense city garden surrounding their home with fruit trees, berry bushes, strawberry plants, vegetables and melons, and even a grape arbor. He sold his produce from the back of his truck on weekends. Over time, he invested in property on the Main Street in town and built a small neighborhood market where he sold his goods and other groceries.

The garden and its riches were a family affair as much as holidays, celebrations and wakes. I remember my brother and I taking the city bus to my grandparent's house (Mom didn't learn to drive until she was in her 50's) to help pick the ripened crops during the peak growing season of the summer. Nana and Mom canned bushels upon bushels of fruit, vegetables, jams and preserves to keep us well fed during the winter months. Mom stored her canned goods in the "fruit cellar" sectioned off in a corner of our basement. (I developed an obsessive fear of spiders that began in that old fruit cellar when I accidentally locked myself in. They still creep me out to this day).

My parents always lived within their means by practicing responsible ways to economize. They taught my brother and me the value of saving and planning for the future. I wish I had followed their example less erratically in my life. This is another thing Alice and I share:

> *"She generally gave herself very good advice,*
> *(though she very seldom followed it)."*
>
> -Lewis Carroll, Alice's Adventures in Wonderland

I know that hard work is worth doing if it preserves my assets, provides for my future and builds a sustainable revenue stream. It is good advice for anyone embarking on an entrepreneurial journey.

My maternal side of our extended family was distinctly different from Dad's family and yet the fundamental principles of ethics and accountability were the same. Mom had fifteen siblings and of the eight boys, all but one grew up to be an independent business owner. Of her seven sisters, three of them were also entrepreneurs. With that many siblings, all vying for their rightful spot in the family hierarchy, they learned some tough lessons about competition. It's no wonder when opportunity lent itself, they chose the road to independence and became business owners.

Child number thirteen, my mom Rita, was only seven years old when her mother passed away shortly after giving birth to her sixteenth child. She had to grow up fast. Older siblings were accountable for guiding the younger children and managing the large household. For example, meal preparation required planning and optimal efficiency. There were no fast-food restaurants, microwave ovens or dishwashers to lend a hand.

My grandpa, titled "P.A." (*the initials*) by his children, ran a tight ship. From the eldest to the youngest, each child knew his or her role and not only was held responsible for accomplishing the tasks but realized at an early age, the importance those actions had on the family unit.

Grandpa was a shrewd businessman. He raised his

large family in a small town in western New York, where he owned a bowling alley, hardware store, plumbing and heating company and farm. Over time, he also acquired several pieces of property within the Rochester and Buffalo, New York area. He groomed his children to work within his establishments, teaching them the skills they would need when he wanted to expand his empire and prepared them to become self-sufficient.

Employer Accountability

As soon as I hire people to work for me, my business must adjust to those new dynamics that are inherent. I must never lose sight that accountability is a two-way street. Yes, I am paying for the work rendered; however, I have an obligation to be a living example of the standards I want my employees to uphold. This is shown by how I dress for work and utilize my time while on the premises. There should be no difference in the level of respect and courtesy I verbally communicate to my employee, vendor or customer.

It begins with the little things when interacting with employees:

- Give my full attention when in conversation with someone
- Deal with issues when they happen
- Say 'thank you' and mean it
- Smile more
- Remember holidays and birthdays and make them special appreciation days

- Ask for opinions and feedback and then seriously consider what has been shared

- Laugh

- Encourage self-improvement

- Educate

- Say 'thank you.' *(I repeat!)*

My employees are so much more than just the necessary cogs in the wheel that keeps the machinery of my business running. They significantly impact its image. If they are discontent, without direction or become unproductive, then my business must be showing those same signs to my customers and prospects.

Jack Stack, the founder and CEO of SRC Holdings, a company comprised of more than thirty-five separate companies, wrote a book about the power of utilizing open-book management and accountability standards. He talks about the importance for us to recognize the effects of what our employees and we do on the job. "It doesn't even matter whether the work is good, bad or indifferent, unless acknowledged for what we do, we will just stop caring."[3]

I find the importance of weekly team meetings with staff essential to maintaining a well-balanced and positive working environment. Even at times when the business may be struggling, these meetings are a valuable communication process that shares the bigger picture of the business's health and how it relies on contributions from its workers. This is the time for me to fill the role of leader, not a boss. I spend seventy-five percent of the time just listening. However, it is important that I keep to the agenda and within the allotted time scheduled. It is my job to inspire them to be motivated.

There are many theories on how to hire the right person for the right job. Too often, under the pressure to quickly fill that vacant seat, the temptation is to just settle for the candidate that is the most readily available for the least amount of money. This only leads to continual turnover, lost time and the expense of re-training and adapting to yet another personality. A constant turn-over in staff is not only costly in dollars but it also weakens the synergy of an experienced and familiar team.

I learned a hiring system from thought leader, author and business/life coach, Jeff Burrows that I have adapted to my specific needs.[4] It has served me exceptionally well over the years, especially with *AERIN, Inc.* From defining the position to be filled with accuracy, composing the advertisement, recruiting, screening candidates, interviewing, and initiating the offer—each step is critical. There are no shortcuts to success. A hiring system developed in advance helps me recruit the right person for the right position.

Anna Johannson, columnist for "Inc. Magazine," lists hiring employees as the number one challenge many small businesses face.[5] Aside from healthcare concerns, it is the related costs above and beyond the salary of the position that puts a strain on the business's bottom line. The increase in payroll taxes, employee benefits, the training, and required additional equipment for the position can leave a company cash poor.

A position agreement should be drawn up that both the employee and employer sign. It is a clear understanding of the commitments both parties agree to uphold. I employ people who will share my purpose.

One of my responsibilities as the leader in my business is to inspire my employees to remain motivated to achieve their personal level of excellence despite the day-to-day challenges of the job. Consideration of self-management, organizational skills and interpersonal relationship skills need to be taken seriously. An employee guidebook is developed to include all staffing-related policies, such as those seemingly simple things: lunch breaks, personal leave, dress codes, conduct and the like, to name a few.

Another trap I can stumble into as a small business owner is assuming employees should be "Minnie ME's[6]," doing everything I want done, exactly the way I would do it and completed according to my timetable. Even worse than this is for me to take the attitude, "I'm better off doing 'it' myself if I want it done right." The moment an individual becomes part of my workforce, they should clearly know what responsibilities are assigned to them and how their position influences other team members and impacts the overall business. I must give them a chance to do it with their own style provided it is respectful to the company guidelines. Functioning as a team, people can lean upon each other's strengths.

Now the Queen of Hearts practiced that her way was the

the *ONLY* way:

"It is better to be feared than loved." – *The* Queen

-Lewis Carroll, Alice's Adventures in Wonderland)

This might work for some people, but I have never found fear and intimidation a healthy way to live. In the 2010 Disney movie remake, "Alice in Wonderland," the Red Queen's subjects went to extreme lengths to make their features distorted to fashionably fit–in with the Queen's disproportionately big head: long noses, elephant ears, pointy chins– to name a few. That certainly back-fired when truth of the falsehoods came out and the fake body parts started falling off the people.

Whenever possible, the work environment is a welcoming place for employees. Good lighting and a comfortable workspace that is clean and free of clutter makes for a pleasant experience. Lunch and break times are respected. Vacation time and personal day policies are carefully defined and fairly enforced.

Most everyone is aware that the responsibilities that go along with child-care, school events, or elder-care can be stressful at times. This means my business might take a back-seat to an employee's family needs. The on-going challenge is not to just have a warm body filling-in for someone but a person skilled enough to do the job correctly and maintain company standards.

Train people to be able to fill multiple roles in a pinch increases efficiency. It's all in the numbers: *5 employees minus 1 employee (out with sick child) equals 20% loss in productivity.*

Get creative and come up with alternative solutions. For example, provide flexible scheduling so a parent can take an extended lunch hour or time out of the day to attend a school event. If the school closes because of inclement weather, coloring books and puzzles, and the availability of an unused conference room or work space can be a simple solution for the displaced child.

In all the years I managed personnel, I cannot remember any incident where an employee took advantage of my generosity. Sometimes, it's all about simply doing the right thing just because you can and it's the right thing to do. Showing employees that you are committed to their health and peace of mind becomes their motivation to achieve higher standards of performance.

Customer Accountability

Accountability is as much a moral obligation in business as it is in the way I live my life outside of work. I am genuine when I understand that the essence of service to others is placing others above me and my needs. I think people inherently are born to be salespeople: From learning as babies to cry to be picked up, to helping a favorite teacher correct papers for unlimited passes out of study hall, to convincing a spouse that a new sofa is a necessary cure for back pain – we all become agents of persuasion. Selling is a learned art but it doesn't mean the seller doesn't have a conscience.

A successful business needs to be profitable. If it hasn't a steady stream of customers willing to buy, it isn't a business.

Selling became more about my credibility and expertise when I learned the difference from focusing on product rather than on the underlying needs of my customer. The key word here, is "underlying."

For many years, I was under the patronizing delusion that the customer is always right. But if that is the case, then what does he need me for? It is my expertise that I continue to hone and elevate that becomes the accountability factor. It is my duty to make it worthy of whatever fee I charge. It may very well mean my dispelling what the customer thinks he wants by showing him what he really needs to reach his goals.

I am the expert. My 30 years of experience and training is valuable. I may run the risk of losing the customer but at least I am genuine. There is no point for me to spend excessive time and energy trying to win the sale when it really isn't destined to be mine to win in the first place.

This goes together with commitments to provide and maintain a high standard of service. I hear many businesses claim to provide exceptional service because they know that is what the customer expects. It is presented like a special gift to the world, the birthday present a child can't wait to unwrap. The products or services offered come in a beautiful package of promises and claims, then tied together with a ribbon of guaranteed on-time, every-time service.

I have found that customer service is more than just a claim. What makes my customer service extraordinarily mine and mine alone? It must be the authentic side of 'me.' What is the differentiator between me and my competitors? I go beyond to become extraordinary.

Sometimes as a promotional products distributor, I face situations that fall outside of my control. For example, I guarantee on-time delivery for print and promotional products that I sell if customer art files and proof approvals are within the pre-production phase and specified guidelines. If a product doesn't reach the destination in the time promised, the responsibility falls on my shoulders to make things right by my customer, even if the delivery carrier is responsible for the delay due to weather. It becomes *my* cost of doing business.

I also believe that achieving enduring relationships with customers is dependent upon establishing a foundational understanding between us equivalent to an honor code. Before any major project gets under way, I utilize a written proposal defining the customer's need and the products and/or services required. After reviewing the proposal for any complex orders or consulting services, it is prudent to acknowledge the agreement in writing.

Here are a few considerations:

- Outline of process from customer authorization to final delivery of product or service.

- Detailed description of the product requested

- Cost of shipping and handling or any other itemized costs not included within the standard price of the product

- Any information the customer must provide to initiate the work order

- Shipping and billing information (if applicable)

- Credit card information

- Pre-Payment or down-payment

- Quantities ordered, colors, sizes, styles

- Disclaimers, if appropriate

- The expected (guaranteed) completion date of project or delivery of goods

Community Accountability

Partaking in community activities is an important ingredient towards living a life of abundance. It allows the barriers that might normally divide people to disappear with a common desire to help others. It provides the entrepreneur with a new opportunity to interact with people outside the work environment and utilize other skills and talents to move to the forefront.

My love of teaching always attracts me to educational opportunities. I assisted in developing an elementary school mentoring program for the South Burlington School District, South Burlington, Vermont. It targeted children who were either having difficulty in school academically or socially. My role was to help introduce this program to local businesses.

This directly led to my service beginning in 1999 as a commissioner on the *Vermont Commission on National and Community Service,* later renamed *SerVermont.* I was actively involved with this commission for the next 10 years. Governor appointed, this commission's responsibility was to oversee the AmeriCorps and VISTA programs in the state as well as be a "voice" for other Vermont non-profit organizations.

It was a humbling experience. So much is done in the name of service in this country and I learned that most of us live outside the scope of the struggles and barriers the caretakers of our society face every day. My desire to work with non-profits prompted me to do some serious homework to better understand the internal workings of each organization I served. Non-profits, despite the name, must be profitable. They are subject to regulations and scrutiny that the typical for-profit businesses may not endure.

I have met some entrepreneurs who formed a not-for-profit business based solely upon a passion for helping others in need. Although their intent was good and noble, it was not enough to be successful. They needed more than just hard work and dedication. Volunteers and donors would come and go, sometimes creating challenges beyond measure.

Non-profits, just like any other business, need a sustainable and sufficient cash flow to survive as well as strong leadership and management skills. They often fail to realize that they have a tremendous amount of competition. Many other non-profit businesses are vying for the same donations from the same individuals and businesses. I recommend entrepreneurs research their options carefully.

Whether for-profit or non-profit, I believe a business should have a purpose beyond just making money. That passion for what I do in my life contributes to the legacy left for those who follow in my footsteps. I can change the world by moving that handful of sand, one day at a time. Whenever I tap into my strengths I've learned from past experiences that it reinforces what I can achieve.

Staying Sane in Wonderland

> "'But I don't want to go among mad people,' Alice
> remarked.
> 'Oh, you can't help that,' said the Cat: 'We're all mad here.
> I'm mad. You're mad.'
> 'How do you know I'm mad?' said Alice.
> 'You must be,' said the Cat, 'or you wouldn't have come
> here.'"
>
> --Lewis Carroll, *Alice's Adventures in Wonderland*

Sanity is directly related to my adaptability to change. Too often, I hear myself bemoaning, "This isn't part of the plan."

Back to *Annie's Honor Snacks*---The empty snack boxes were incredibly light and durable and were designed to stack nicely on top of each other. It seemed easy enough—insert the dividers and fill the boxes with assorted snacks. We never considered the differences in how the packaging and shape of the individual snacks could create new problems for us. The bags of chips had to be carefully tilted so they would lay below the top edge of the box. Otherwise, they would be crushed when stacking the boxes. That sacrificed room inside the box for other kinds of snacks to fit. Some businesses had to be delivered two boxes each trip, just to accommodate their chip and popcorn consumption.

Also, remember those "picnic bonnets" that I lovingly designed to go over the contents of snack boxes? They interfered with the inter-locking corners that attached one box to another. Most ended up in my rag-bag.

It never entered my mind that the efficiency of the transportation system I devised would be challenged. Once we got the boxes stacked, we had difficulty keeping the tower of boxes from shifting and falling over in the back of the van. All it took was a bump in the road, going uphill or maneuvering corners to upset the load. Our stacks had to be limited to five-high, shrinking the total capacity per van. This often required an extra trip back to home-base, cutting a big chunk out of delivery time. We never did come up with an ideal system.

While Vermont may be best known for its skiing, fall foliage and maple syrup, its residents know only too well, the fickleness of its weather. Vermont does have some delightfully warm days. It didn't take much for a candy bar to melt in a closed and locked vehicle without the air conditioning running. Certain items such as pies, cream-filled Devil-Dogs™ and glazed donuts melted or developed condensation in the heat.

Winter offered its own challenges causing our juices to freeze. The mounting snow piles became hazardous and challenging for parking curbside or trying to walk, balance snack boxes and remain upright in the unplowed or icy parking lots.

Delivery delays, ruined inventory and potentially unhappy customers are just not good for any business. People for the most part are pretty understanding if you are genuine and honest. A snow storm is a reasonable delay, but a "late start" that happens repeatedly or a change in delivery day with questionable excuses is never okay.

By 1985, *Annie's Honor Snacks* had become a fully functional business with organized routines in place, a stable and efficient workforce and a loyal customer base. Despite its setbacks, it was now profitable and debt-free. That presented new challenges. It was growing, but I didn't have the manpower or space to accommodate the growth, even with two delivery vehicles and two full-time employees in addition to myself. We could barely keep up with the daily demands of our customers.

I was most fortunate to have ideal employees. They were always reliable, efficient, innovative and impeccably honest. They had been prior students of mine, I attended their high school graduation and continued to remain in contact. We had a comfort level between us that is seldom achieved between employer and employee. And that was my dilemma – I needed to hire more help but how could I be certain that the individual I brought on would be as trustworthy and dependable as I was accustomed?

Remember, my snack service was based upon the honor system. Vetting a new hire carefully was significant because we were handling cash sales. The coin boxes were not under lock and key. Keeping their contents intact and in the correct snack box was critical to maintaining accuracy. I began to realize that as my staffing needs grew, this concern would grow as well.

One choice I considered was to redesign the snack box including a permanent built-in and lockable coin box. I worried that it would have a negative impact upon the honor system that my business was founded on. Would my customers be offended? Was I hurting my brand?

The next dilemma we faced was an urgent need for more room. Our garage and home office space was no longer sufficient. I had increased volume purchases to take advantage of higher volume profit margins but an 18-wheeler driving down our residential street did not make for happy neighbors.

It never occurred to me that it would be an issue until I received a notice to appear before the Town Planning and Zoning Board. I quickly reassessed our situation, took off the blinders and realized our neighbors' perspective. These trucks were too loud, too big, and too disruptive. Now we had to arrange to meet our vendors at designated locations, transfer the products into our vans and cart them back to the house.

Things were getting complicated. Success is a wonderful thing until you realize that growth untamed can be a killer too. A change was brewing.

For the second time in my marriage, things became strained between my husband and me. This time it was *Annie's Honor Snacks*. He was unhappy with the demands of his job and wanted to explore other possibilities. My business was becoming an inconvenience to his ambitions.

He was an excellent golfer and loved the thought of living in a climate where he'd be able to play year-round. Vermont is a small state and he believed his work opportunities were limited. My business was the one thing holding us back from pursuing a better life. If only I was willing to get a "normal" job like him, we could move. Why, I could be a teacher again!

The staffing shortage and the need to invest in more employees, the looming expense of a warehouse and another delivery vehicle just added fuel to the fire. Filled with uncertainty and afraid I would fail undertaking such a massive expansion on my own, I sold *Annie's Honor Snacks.*

> *"But it's no use now," thought poor Alice, 'to pretend to be two people!*
> *Why, there's hardly enough of me left to make one respectable person!'"*
>
> — *Lewis Carroll, Alice's Adventures in Wonderland*

It was the spring of 1986. Within a few months, we put our house on the market. We never did leave Vermont. Instead, we moved into a more affluent neighborhood in South Burlington with the promise of a great school system for our daughter who would be entering kindergarten soon. I bought another business, becoming an associate distributor of *Safeguard Business Systems, Inc.*™ I now owned rights to a lucrative customer base of business in the north-western part of Vermont.

My spouse's unhappiness with his current job once again became the main topic of conversation between us. I started to feel guilty that here I was, living the life of an entrepreneur and building my business while he was miserable working for someone else. We decided to go all in and purchased another piece of the Safeguard distributorship that was available in northeastern Vermont and northern New Hampshire. I was convinced we would make a great husband and wife team and told myself that our newly formed partnership would fortify the fragile framework of our marriage. "Now we can BOTH claim to be independent business owners," I thought. "No worries-- we are going to be just fine."

I know that every decision or indecision I make, large and small, can impact my business success, my life and the lives of the people who surround me. I have learned that I may be willing to make the sacrifices but are they? I could no more convince my husband to buy into my entrepreneurial vision and work ethics than I could get him to agree with me on our lifestyle choices, financial management and need for family commitment.

My first marriage failed after fourteen years. It was a long time coming but I didn't "see" it, and most people outside our home were as equally shocked as I was when he asked for a divorce. I was ashamed at what I saw as my failure to make my marriage work and the pain and distress it put on my daughter. I was overwhelmed with the effects our divorce had on relationships with family, friends, business associates and competitors. Too many secrets and too many deceptions, and our "dynamo team" was no more.

In moments of weakness, like Alice, I have wished I could shut up like a telescope and hide away. Whenever Alice tries to make sense of who she really is and why she ended up in Wonderland, she determines that it must be either herself or the Red King that is responsible. She finally concludes:

> *"He was part of my dream, of course --*
> *but then I was part of his dream, too!"*
> --Lewis Carroll, *Alice in Wonderland*

Blame never got me anywhere. I always had choices that I could act upon or chose to ignore. To me, there is always loss in a divorce-- whether it is monetary or emotional, it is traumatic and has a lasting impact. Even if the changes may be forced and painful, they can also be liberating. Suddenly, I became aware just how those choices I had made in the name of marriage and love affected me on a deeper and more profound level. I could begin to look back and objectively view my past behaviors for what they were and envision how I would guide my future actions.

Once our decision to separate became public, I was shocked and mortified when asked, "So, now what do you plan to do for work?" This assumption that the man would likely control the business infuriated me. In the five years I had owned it, I more than doubled the original base of business I had purchased. I loved my work and I loved the opportunities that were before me. I was not going to conform to society's expectations and give it up just because I was a woman.

My main competitor used our imminent divorce to his advantage by convincing two major banks in the area that renewing their referral agreements with my company was risky. This was a major setback, since the volume of referrals accounted for a significant percentage of my revenue stream.

If this wasn't enough, learning that our personal financial situation was on the verge of disaster, threw me into a tailspin. How did I not see this coming? The "must have" Country Club membership, his new golf clubs, the boat upgrade, car, vacations— the evidence was all there. I had overlooked the past due notices that supposedly crossed in the mail with the payments. I'd heard the song before, but I chose to cover my ears. The money we had earned went out the door as fast as it came in. There was no choice but for us to liquidate our few assets, sell the house to pay off as many of the debts as we could, and start over independently.

> *"The executioner's argument was that you couldn't cut off something's head (Cheshire Cat's) unless there was a trunk to sever it from. He'd never done anything like that in his time of life, and wasn't going to start now.*
> *The King's argument was that anything that had a head, could be beheaded, and you weren't to talk nonsense.*
> *The Queen's argument was that if something wasn't done about it in less than no time, she'd have everyone beheaded all round.*
> *It was this last argument that had everyone looking so nervous."*
> *--Lewis Carroll, Alice's Adventures in Wonderland*

I filled the emptiness I felt inside me by immersing myself in my business. I began reading and studying self-empowerment books and listening to CD's. Not only did I want to be a leader, but I wanted to *feel* like a leader. If I didn't get myself out of the funk I was in, it would destroy what little self-confidence I still had. I *could* change myself. I *would* change myself. I would grow into a stronger-willed woman, empower myself to choose my own path, and be a model my daughter would be proud to call her mom.

I began to strategize on ways to cut or reduce expenditures, increase my revenue stream and build up my assets. I desperately needed access to some ready cash to help me deal with the division of my portion of shared business expenses. Dissolving the business partnership meant two offices instead of one, staffing changes, additional equipment, insurance policies, and accountant and attorney fees. These were over and above the standard operating expenses of the business.

Unfortunately, banks still considered me high risk despite evidence that my part of the business as defined by my contractual agreement as an independent distributor, (and would remain solely in my possession), had continually experienced growth and profitability. *Annie's Honor Snacks* showed a profit when I sold it. Like a few other people, all they saw was a soon-to-be divorced single parent and a woman running a business on her own. I was advised to come back in about a year, and if I was doing well, they might be able to assist me. I was furious.

I took a hard look at my financial picture, and defined the monthly constants for both business and personal, setting up a conservative cash flow projection. From that I could build out a plan of action and a timeline to get myself out of the red.

My immediate attention was focused on finding a new home for my daughter and me that would allow her to be in the same school system. I swallowed my pride and asked my parents for a loan to help subsidize the down payment on the purchase of a small condominium that I would pay back within the next seven years. I traded-in my two-year old car for a less expensive car, cutting my monthly car payment by 40 percent and started clipping coupons for groceries. Baby sitters were an unnecessary expense. If I was invited to an adult-only night out, it had to be on a weekend when my daughter was visiting her father or sleeping over at a friend's house.

As I worked on controlling my personal finances, I recognized the similar need for business owners. When the U.S. economy dipped in the early 1990's, some of the hardest hit areas were in California and the northeast.[1] I saw many small business owners struggling financially to survive and compete with the advancing technology and internet boom.

I came up with an idea to start an association for bookkeepers that could cultivate the continued health of small business. It would advocate sound record-keeping practices and management through an informational and educational network. Emphasis would be placed on understanding and utilizing financial tools such as cash flow, balance sheet, and profit and loss reports to track the monetary health of the business. I would also focus on teaching the basics for installing and setting up some of the top accounting software programs that were preferred in the marketplace.

I decided to redirect my focus on *BKPR, Inc.* (*Bookkeepers Professional Resources Association*), a fledgling operation at the time, to maximize my referral sources and provide the small business community access to bookkeepers willing to adopt the *BKPR Compliance of Standards and Accountability*. In addition, this would be an optional local service I could personally offer to my Safeguard customers. This enterprise and *Annie's Honor Snacks* were alike because it also began from a single concept and expanded from my creativity.

I conducted a survey of my existing customer base and determined that independent professional bookkeepers were a growing profession based upon several trends:

- Increase of home-based businesses

- Need for flexible work schedules

- Availability of affordable enhanced technology

- Emergence of a large population of experienced, highly qualified, unemployed people due to downsizing

- Growing number of women emerging in the workforce.

Small businesses were transitioning from manual to computerized accounting solutions. I realized that bookkeepers could fill a large part of this void by providing a much-needed service only when required. Bookkeepers would be a decisive link between accountants, financial advisors and business owners in the rapidly changing business environment necessitating the changeover from manual to computerized accounting and management solutions.

Both bookkeepers and business owners needed on-going educational opportunities to keep themselves operating at optimal performance. The certification program defined four levels of bookkeeping expertise: basic, intermediate, full-charge and managerial. Certified Public Accountants and qualified, trained independent bookkeepers became my instructors and mentors for a variety of popular accounting software packages and bookkeeping/accounting skill sets. Here was a way I could differentiate myself from my competitors by serving as a resource center of information and services rather than only a purveyor of products.

BKPR served a great purpose for 6 years until once again, I found myself having to choose some significantly dramatic restructuring of my core business or curtail my involvement. I didn't have the foresight or know-how to develop an infrastructure that could sustain the organization if I wasn't the leader. The extra hours I put into the planning and development of curriculum, scheduling and hosting classes and conferences, and marketing efforts began to take its toll.

On its own, the development of a *BKPR* certified program for testing levels of bookkeeping/accounting expertise for members was nearly a full time job as it required extensive research and a special skill set for designing effective test assessments. I was again reminded that no matter how well I plan, the freedom I experience as an entrepreneur always comes with a significant amount of risk and sacrifice.

The greatest gift I got out of *BKPR* was a blossoming relationship with one of its members, George Richard. In case you didn't catch the name similarity, after two years, George and I became a couple and married in 1994. We are still crazily, joyfully building our dream together: a future where we travel to new places, spend quality time with family and friends and have the financial freedom to maintain a comfortable lifestyle of our choosing.

> *"Have I gone mad?*
> *I'm afraid so, but let me tell you something,*
> *the best people usually are."*
>
> — *Lewis Carroll, Alice's Adventures in Wonderland*

Over and Under

The fact that I operated Annie's Honor Snacks primarily on a cash basis miraculously kept that business afloat. I could run to the bank every day with the daily earnings. Friday's deposits paid for vendor deliveries on Monday. My home-based business eliminated a considerable number of over-head expenses but it gave me a false sense of financial security. If the checking account wasn't over-drawn, I could make it another day. If I had a balance of $1000 in the business account after expenses at the end of the month, I was over-joyed. In those days, I didn't have the foresight to erect a solid foundation that could weather a heavy rain storm.

When my uncle pulled out of the partnership I felt going to family for help was not an option. Instead, I withdrew my teacher's retirement account to pay for start up costs and personal debt. I feared my need would be looked upon as evidence of my failure. So, I went to my banker. He gave me a $7,000 loan, sealing the deal with a hand-shake as I didn't have any real collateral. It was not enough. And, the money was soon gone.

Besides the loan payment, other expenses mounted up. In 1982, I became pregnant, and was without the benefits of a teacher's medical insurance nor coverage through my husband's job. We didn't have a cushion to fall back on and had to depend on cutting-back expenses whenever we could.

We relied on our wood stove to save on heating costs. My husband patched the holes of our eight-year-old car with plywood after he put his foot through the rusted-out floor pushing down on the brake pedal. Between the mortgage and other expenses, we were flat broke with a new business.

Then my husband lost his managerial position due to poor performance. *Annie's Honor Snacks* couldn't support us on its own merit. He took a job in computer sales and for a period he stayed focused and was performing well. The job was paid on straight commissions however, and we never could depend on what his paycheck would be from one month to the next.

To keep us solvent, we negotiated a loan for $5,000 from a friend at twenty percent interest. Crazy, huh? Desperation and pride can do funny things to people. Whatever capital you think you need to get your business up and running, think again. At the very least, I suggest you more than double that amount. At all times, I have learned I should keep a minimum of six months' cash reserve to cover all operating expenses, and that includes paying myself.

Having a second source of income eventually paid off and we could breathe again. Every day, I focused on acquiring new accounts for *Annie's Honor Snacks*. My assistant focused on making the deliveries on time and made to order. We began to make headway. We carefully analyzed how we could be more efficient and expend less energy. I got my top suppliers to bill me monthly instead of weekly and negotiated for better rates.

Diversification can be very profitable but any type of growth or expansion also has its pitfalls and should be seriously studied before an investment is made. For instance, when I expanded my service to include the heavy-duty coffee machines, they came with a significant price tag. The deal I offered customers was to provide the machines for free with the agreement that all coffee supplies would be purchased from me.

It took some time to be able to determine my break-even point because each location had different drinking habits. Now I had something else to service and deliver. With a limited staff, it meant extra hours for me to set up and maintain the machines in addition to driving sales and signing up new customers.

As much as I wanted to build the coffee service, my limited capital didn't allow me to make the significant investment in equipment, product and marketing. Other coffee services that popped-up in the area were focused on the market and acquired the financial backing they needed. They planned, orchestrated and expanded methodically and purposefully. I didn't have the experience to do this and lacked the wisdom to find the right people to advise me.

On the other hand, when I expanded *Annie's Honor Snacks* to include a lunch catering service, that held more promise. A local deli prepared the foods and we picked the lunches up and delivered them as part of our regularly scheduled routes. This additional service for my customers provided me with another revenue stream without incurring overhead costs and minimal additional time invested. Business owners and managers took advantage of utilizing employees' lunch breaks to run their weekly staff meetings. Employees appreciated having a free lunch at the owner's expense.

I had enough sense however, to hire a knowledgeable certified public accountant who knew how to legitimately prepare our tax returns. As my needs changed over the years, I learned from *Annie's Honor Snacks* that whenever a significant financial shift occurs in the business, I need to meet with my accountant. The reason why some people can write "CPA" after their names is because they are required to maintain a continued level of training in their field and they are knowledgeable about changes in tax law and regulations. I have been audited by the Internal Revenue Service three times. Each time I had my accountant beside me. It provided me with great peace of mind to know everything was in order.

I bought into the notion that 'more' is better. Personal success meant more money and more status. The entrepreneur mindset translates this into more diverse product offerings, the latest technology expenditures, mergers and acquisitions, awards and recognition—all signs of success and prosperity-- or so it seems. These goals can become an entrepreneur's undoing. Growth is great and comes in many forms but it's called "growing pains" for a reason.

Knowing when it is the right time to make that next jump will ultimately be the critical factor. Money, marketing and management must be both envisioned and capable of execution. If I chase after a new dream without a good dose of realistic planning, I risk losing myself and my purpose.

"If you drink much from a bottle marked 'poison,' it is almost certain to disagree with you, sooner or later." (Alice)
—*Lewis Carroll, Alice's Adventures in Wonderland*

Some lessons are just hard to learn. I've never been at a loss for ideas. *Annie's Honor Snacks* was just the beginning. With each subsequent business endeavor, I have had to reign myself in from starting too many projects and making commitments to others that hurt me financially or increased my stress level. I've learned to be more patient.

When I set a goal, I develop benchmarks along the way to measure my progress and keep me on course. This has lessened the odds of having undesired results by keeping me focused. It is too easy to give up on an activity that isn't providing immediate gratification and jump to another one.

In hindsight, when I formed the professional bookkeepers' association (*BKPR*), I should have pursued my vision of developing the organization. I should have sought out good advisors experienced in membership organizations who could mentor me. My feeble attempts to find investors and explore franchising possibilities were discouraging after the first and second rejection. Right away, I thought I was lacking and my ideas were outside my capabilities, or the plan itself was unworthy of investment. Unlike the coffee service for *Annie's Honor Snacks*, *BKPR's* uniqueness set it distinctly apart from other enterprises by filling an immediate need and much desired service to the small business community.

Being solely on my own and with only a modest amount of money to invest, I abandoned the dream. One thing that *Annie's Honor Snacks* and *BKPR* did have in common was evidence that my old habits and belief systems die hard. I was proud to be a woman and entrepreneur but my lack of self-esteem and with no one willing to share the struggle, my legs just turned to jelly.

I often wonder what it would have been like if I had been stronger and more determined to make BKPR work. But, as the Queen tells Alice:

"It's a poor sort of memory that only works backward."

--*Lewis Carroll, Alice's Adventures in Wonderland*

If I knew back then what I know today, I would launch BKPR as a network-distribution company. My company's core products would be tutorial books for free-lance professional bookkeepers. They would be comprised of *BKPR's* four developmental levels of bookkeeping/accounting standards for small businesses. In addition, it would have seminar training guides and how-to workbooks for end-users. An on-line presence would take advantage of the internet's power of connection and convenience.

The beauty behind this type of business compared to a franchise or my Safeguard™ distributorship is the low overhead. Members join with a minimal amount of capital outlay. They make money depending on their involvement through commissions received through product sales or by building a team of other sales representatives. They also have the option to just be consumers and utilize the products and training for their own personal development. As more people are involved, opportunity for expansion into other geographical areas can happen at a faster pace.

For people with the entrepreneurial spirit but lack experience in direct sales, the availability of a strong support team and mentors would be a greatly appealing benefit. Going it alone as an entrepreneur is tough—I know because I have been there.

Misinformed people still think that direct marketing companies can all be lumped into a category of network marketing "get rich-quick" schemes by brainwashing friends and family to purchase over-priced and over-valued products. I have found that it depends upon the ethics of not only the company itself but the people representing it. The business structure matters little if the owner and/or representatives are untrustworthy and deceptive. It still comes down to being selective when choosing what people or entities with whom you want to associate.

Knowing when to say no is just as important to an entrepreneur as is the willingness to take risks. I try to test the water more carefully, noting the temperature, but also whether it is clear or murky and what might be moving under the surface. Whatever is swimming down there, will it nourish me or make me its dinner?

Run Around or Get Run Over

"If I had a world of my own, everything would be nonsense.
Nothing would be what it is, because everything would be
what it isn't.
And contrary wise, what is, it wouldn't be.
And what it wouldn't be, it would. You see?" (The Hatter)
        -Lewis Carroll, Alice's Adventures in Wonderland

Alice gets quite good at adapting to the various situations she gets herself into. Between magic potions and cakes and coercing herself into the Wonderland affairs, she manages to always persevere. After all, she can pinch herself and wake up if things get out of hand.

Life, of course, is not so accommodating. Entrepreneurs sometimes find their best solution to unwanted situations is deliberately choosing detours rather than facing all the traffic on the express way. When I have found myself in such circumstances, I need to be careful not to get too side-tracked and lose my focus on my fundamental priorities.

I was certain that I needed a storefront for my business so I could maintain my foothold in the marketplace. The visual presence would indicate an image of permanence and stability. In time, despite efforts to multi-purpose office space for hosting meetings and other events to justify the overhead expense, I opted for the home-based office.

This reasoning was sound for several reasons. Customers rarely came to my office to conduct business. Fifty percent of useable office space housed our color-coded filing system that contained customer order history and print samples. The 7,000 accumulated records stored on twelve shelving units three feet wide by fifteen inches deep, took up a significant amount of floor space. All remaining area was occupied by work stations, office equipment, marketing materials and supplies.

I began working on finding alternative solutions for records management suitable to my budget restrictions. I tried software applications combined with a high-end scanner to automate our filing system. I found it was time-intensive having to complete five to ten required document scans per order and enter the appropriate customer tracking information into the computer. Our pre-existing customer management software was incompatible. By moving my business into my home I freed up some capital to invest in marketing and better office efficiency.

The sentiment that home-based businesses aren't seriously considered to be "real" businesses has changed over time largely due to the freedom that has come with technology. A home-based business may be comprised of a 'solo-preneur', or freelance agents or employees working from their homes or other locations. In fact, The Small Business Administration claims that more than half of all U.S. businesses are based out of an owner's home.[1] Sometimes people assume that these businesses are fledgling operations with limited long-term earning potential. This is far from the truth.

Just look at companies such as Mary Kay, Apple Computer and the Ford Motor Company— they originated as home-based businesses.   Ben Gran, a freelance writer for Fortune 500 companies stated on the *incfile.com* blog that 70 percent of home-based businesses are successful within three years of founding, compared with only 30 percent of regular businesses. A surprising 20 percent of these home-based businesses make $100K-$500K per year — and that's a very comfortable income.[2]

Starting an entrepreneurial adventure based at home will offer unique challenges that if overlooked can turn 'home-sweet-home' into a detention center. It is necessary for me to conscientiously balance space, time and commitment between the daily demands of business and life so that they serve each other.

A home-based business, especially if it provides product, has a way of spilling over into personal space as if it has a life of its own. Boxes of product once stacked in the corner of the living room can eventually overflow into the hallway. What once was a dining room table becomes the central office work space. Kids are relegated to their rooms or outside because a parent needs quiet to be able to concentrate on the business task at hand. Neighbors may get annoyed by an increase in mail/package deliveries to the house and 'man's best friend' becomes an inconvenience because it needs to be let out or barks too much at the wrong times.

If I let my home-based business control me, I will never be free from its unending demands. The business will always be there and there is always something that needs doing. Nights or weekends become time to catch-up on the accounting— And what about the flip-side? If I allow my home life to take control, the distractions might get the laundry done, the beds made, the leaves raked and the trash taken out while phone calls to prospects get put-off for another day.

Operating a home-based business provides exceptional flexibility for the disciplined entrepreneur that segregates its business operations into a well-organized space and adheres to a dedicated work schedule with the least amount of disruption to the home. My experience working from both my home and leased office space in a variety of scenarios has given me the confidence to advise other entrepreneurs who are faced with this decision.

At one stage, the entire basement of my home was remodeled for my business. We installed a handicapped accessible entrance for employees and infrequent visitors in anticipation of future needs. When work was over for the day, I would go upstairs and close the basement door. This was helpful in keeping business separate from my personal life.

Most days, whether I have appointments or not, I get up in the morning, shower and dress as if I am seeing customers. It is important for me to have the right mindset to be able to work efficiently. By immersing myself in my professional role, I am more in-tune to the activities that are happening around me and can respond thoughtfully and with purpose.

It has taken me years to have the discipline to "turn-off" that work switch. I'm a poor sleeper and have spent countless nights in the office working on something I just can't allow myself to put off until tomorrow. What I intend to be a half hour turns into two or three hours. Allowing myself enough time to get the job done or finding outside help or reassigning the task to someone else, should be my first consideration.

I also have found these midnight forays to produce some of my best work. When that is the case, I offer myself a compromise that allows me to sleep-in an extra hour or two the next morning or a mid-day break to catch a "cat-nap." This keeps me alert and refreshed. If not, it is a sure way to experience "burn-out."

Another challenge for the home-based business is contacting, meeting and building professional relationships. I like the convenience of email and text messaging because it is quick and convenient. However, there is an underlying feeling of disconnect from humanity. It is easy for communications to be misinterpreted or considered impersonal. Being able to use real-time face-to-face and hear a voice's inflections is significant in building a tangible relationship. An alternative is on-line conferencing services.

I make every effort to go out of my way to meet prospective customers in person whenever possible. I give serious thought into where and when to meet. It is easy to become isolated when operating from a home office. Avoiding outside human contact makes it more difficult to relate to others on a professional level, carry-on intelligent conversations or express personal emotions and insights effectively. I must ask myself: "What image do I personify to accurately portray the personality, professionalism and credibility of my business?"

An ideal place for me to have a professional meeting is at my prospect's place of work. This accomplishes several things: I get a feeling of the ambiance of the workplace and a sense of its productivity. It gives insight as to other ways I might service the customer. Family pictures hung on the wall, certificates of achievement, golf clubs propped in the corner, all provide openings to engage in friendly conversation. Meeting on my prospect's turf allows her/him to feel more relaxed and in control.

Oftentimes, people prefer not to meet at their office because it is too distracting or inconvenient. If they are home-based as I am, they might be uncomfortable having a stranger come to their home. I try to find a public place to meet. What I intend to accomplish at the meeting determines the location and the time I invest in my preparation and the marketing materials I need to have at my disposal.

I judge people by my first impression of them. If I am trying to establish a professional relationship with someone, I realize I need to look and act the part. People shouldn't have to guess whether I am sincere or dependable. I should personify that image to gain the opportunity to prove it. I look for these traits in others:

- Are they on time?
- Are they dressed professionally?
- Have they prepared for our meeting?

I have nothing against tattoos (show me yours and I'll show you mine) or face piercings or blue jeans, but depending upon the professional business environment, a certain dress etiquette is necessary. If I'm interviewing someone with hopes of that person becoming a customer or a referral source, those first impressions will count.

My home-based business has tax ramifications. I designate a specific space in my house that I can solely use for the business — It is not shared in any way with our personal living space. I take photos of it, measure the dimensions of the space and calculate the percentage of our entire household expenses that are needed for it to function. In addition, we record and accurately itemize all expenses related to our business such as plane fares, mileage, professional meals out, on-going training and logoed business apparel. This information will be valuable when it is time to file tax returns.

I operate a home-based business for a myriad of reasons yet at the basis of them all is the flexibility it gives me. I can circumvent barriers that get in my way much easier than if I am locked into a lease. If there's a down-turn in the economy, I can scale down. If business is booming, I can out-source help on an as-needed basis in areas that require specialization. I have those added benefits of the personal and financial perks that come with working from my home.

If I persevere in reaching my goals, I can take a few back roads and shortcuts to avoid those traffic jams and still get to the destination in one piece—Who knows? It may even be in record time. While in Wonderland, the King tells Alice:

"Begin at the beginning and go till you come to the end:
then stop. — Lewis Carroll, *Alice's Adventures in Wonderland*

IT S ABOUT TIME

"No wonder your late. Why this watch is exactly two days slow." (The Hatter)
— Lewis Carroll, *Alice's Adventures in Wonderland*

A favorite cliché people use is "time flies." We have come to allow our waking time to be fractured just like time in Alice's Wonderland delightfully portrayed at the Mad Hatter's tea party.

In the story, the Queen of Hearts accused the Hatter of wasting 'Time,' and time happens to be a person. Time is punishing the Hatter because he offended him and made the Hatter's broken watch, (which only tells the day of the month), stick at six o'clock. All 'time,' is tea 'time.' All the places around the great table are set with several tea pots and dishes of food and silverware. No one has 'Time' to clean the dishes. When they want a clean plate, they rotate to another seat.

Let's not forget about the White Rabbit. He is the catalyst that got Alice into Wonderland in the first place. He is constantly anxious: checking his watch, as he dashes off, muttering, "Oh my ears and whiskers, how late it's getting!" Alice chases off after him with little thought or concern for where she's going and what to do when she gets there.

An abuser of time, I have occasionally been reluctant to adapt and change mediocre habits despite the unsatisfactory results that might carry into my life and my businesses. In truth, I often have had no difficulty blaming others for the undesirable outcomes that result from my lost time.

I hear employers complain that today's employees have no work ethics. I hear employees complain that their boss is never satisfied. Both seem to feel stressed-out and undervalued. Even Alice preferred to deal with the extremes that existed in Wonderland instead of dealing with her feelings of insecurities and frustrations she had experienced living in the real world.

"Numerous studies show that job stress is far and away the major source of stress for American adults and that it has escalated progressively over the past few decades. Increased levels of job stress as assessed by the perception of having little control but lots of demands have been demonstrated to be associated with increased rates of heart attack, hypertension and other disorders."[1]

The 'could have', 'should have' reflections of past choices exist only to haunt my dreams. Successful entrepreneurs take full responsibility for their actions and the energy they put into it. They continuously look for ways to inspire themselves by emulating the habits of people they admire and respect. Part of my adaptability to make changes in the workplace is my willingness to invent and reinvent myself when the need arises.

Even the Hatter points out to Alice that saying what she means and meaning what she says are not the same thing. Efficiency doesn't come naturally to me. It must be learned. It is not just distractions; it is often self-imposed delays and detours that keep me from accomplishing what I've set out to do.

When my daughter was still an infant, I would strap her baby-carrier on me while I packed snack boxes or worked at the computer. I loved having her close to me, and once asleep she'd sleep through anything! As she got older, we set up a space in the center of our assembly line tables where she could watch us and play with her toys at the same time. Sometimes she went on deliveries with me. I'd take the short, easy routes since I had to allow time for getting her into and out of the car seat, and the backpack. She had to be fed when she was hungry and diapers needed changing.

It didn't take me long to realize how wasteful I was being with my time. I knew I wasn't cut out to be a delivery route driver, but I was doing it. What I needed and thrived on was adult interaction and the challenge of earning new accounts. Of course, I loved being a mom, but I was a better person when I could challenge my entrepreneurial self.

I enrolled my daughter into a neighborhood daycare three afternoons a week to free up my time. It was good for her to be with other children and it was good for me. I no longer had the excuse to just stay home in my blue jeans and t-shirt, and distract myself with housekeeping activities.

Sometimes inefficiencies are not so apparent. It may be the extended lunch hour to include watching a favorite show on TV or running to the supermarket for the evening's dinner. These evasions, these inefficiencies happen for a reason. For some people, the case may prove to be they are unhappy with their home life, are unsuited for the career they've settled into or simply unhappy with the results they have achieved.

Most often, I create the roadblocks that prevent me from achieving that degree of excellence I am striving to reach. I become the source of my own unhappiness. The clock never stops ticking. Constant change, though frightening and tumultuous, provides me opportunities for growth and understanding. After all, can someone dive into a rabbit hole and come out unchanged?

Alice: "How long is forever?"
The White Rabbit: "Sometimes just one second."

-Lewis Carroll, Alice's Adventures in Wonderland

To be a true entrepreneur, I must balance my time between fulfilling roles as leader, manager and marketer. Like it or not, as the founder and owner of my business, I'm "IT." Numero Uno-- The Big Cheese-- The Brand Identifier. I am my business and my business is me. It is ultimately my responsibility to effectively and consistently communicate my business's true purpose for existing. Effective communication can provide inspiration for employees to become leaders and managers while differentiating my business from other potential "look-a-likes."

Finding others that will efficiently use their time, energy and talents within my business, means I can gain a greater capacity to objectively use my time to enlarge my personal perspective. As Michael Gerber's *E-Myth*™ principle states, I should spend less time working in my business and instead focus my talents and creativity working on it.[2] I can begin to live each day in the present with anticipation for the journey it offers and with a clarity that is unencumbered by just my need for activity. My passion and creativity to adapt and evolve as a person and as an entrepreneur will move my business further along the pathway towards my vision.

No one can effectively maximize the roles of leader, manager and marketer all the time or all at once. Recognizing that I can't do it all is the first step. I find myself constantly doing a 'self-check-up." Am I focusing on putting my strengths and talents first or am I using my time and effort on things that need doing? Or, am I the right person to be doing it? In the worst case, I'm deluding myself that I am the only one who can get the job done right.

The second step is identifying and recruiting the right person or persons to help me develop my business. In theory, this may be easier said than it is to accomplish. The result can be the difference in investing in my business or just keep throwing money away on time-wasting inefficiencies.

"Take some more tea, "The March Hare said to Alice.
"I've had nothing yet,' Alice replied in an offended tone,
'so I can't take more.'
'You mean you can't take less.' said the Hatter.
'It's very easy to take more than nothing."
— *Lewis Carroll, Alice's Adventures in Wonderland*

A significant part of my business growth for *AERIN, Inc.* can be attributed to four business acquisitions I transacted over a fifteen-year period to increase and diversify my customer base and geographical footprint. Each one presented its own unique challenges. The biggest challenge was the allocation of time and who to entrust with it.

By far, the most demanding undertaking was the purchase of the Vermont-New Hampshire Safeguard™ distributorship in its entirety in 2001. Separate from the research and development, contract negotiations and sales agreement necessary for the transfer of ownership, I had to contend with complicated and unpredictable setbacks resulting in the integration of 7,000 customer records and software modifications, along with the assimilation of telephone and computer services. Meanwhile, I had to keep my existing business functioning smoothly and without interruption and bolster an active and visible presence for both states.

Let me tell you about my painfully unavoidable experience administrating a 1.2 million-dollar business and the seemingly inescapable forces at work that kept interfering with my progress. Two of the three full-time employees operating from the New Hampshire office were excited to join my team. Both were seasoned employees having worked for my predecessor for an excess of five years and knew the customer management software, order processing and product lines as well as I did.

And then tragedy struck. With only two weeks into my territory purchase, my star sales manager died unexpectedly. This left me with no outside sales force residing in New Hampshire. Over the course of the next two years, I hired and lost four people attempting to fill that sales position. George and I exhausted ourselves trying to service both states putting in 12-16 hour days. The additional expense of overnights and windshield-time to cover New Hampshire divided time we had reserved for our Vermont customer development. The existence of a personal life outside of the business had frozen in time.

> *"Now, here, you see, it takes all the running you can do, to keep in the same place.*
> *If you want to get somewhere else, you must run at least twice as fast as that!"*
> *--Lewis Carroll, Through the Looking Glass*

My business should serve a life's purpose, and not evolve into a position of meaningless servitude. Small business owners often cut corners by trying to do all the work instead of finding someone to help them. Following this pattern of behavior for too long can become fatal to the business's well-being.

Dramatis Personae

Building lasting and meaningful relationships with employees is one of the most challenging and most rewarding aspect of running a successful business. I wish I could say I have the magic formula for hiring the right person for the right job. All I know, is that I eventually incorporated a process for *AERIN, Inc.* that brought me the results I desired. Not only can a business survive by using a thoughtful, measurable hiring process, the changes can lead to an increase in vitality and well-being where all the characters involved can revisit the business's vision and purpose and reaffirm their roles.

One of the biggest headaches an employer faces is having an employee that is always surrounded in drama *AND* is highly productive at the same time. It is so easy to fall into a trap of believing that the business can't survive without that person. It can survive, of course. Where personal relationships are more difficult to control, a business environment provides endless opportunities to create blueprints for constructing a stable work environment and prepare for the probable changes in staffing.

Alice wasn't the only one caught up in a pool of salt-water created by her own giant tears. Birds and mice and other creatures fell in and struggled to find land and get dry. It wasn't so much that she was insensitive as it was her self-assured ignorance that kept her from being respected by the other characters.

For childlike Alice, an allowable view of the world may consist of a universe with the child at its center. As the child grows and matures into an adult, that world view needs to change to accommodate people and things beyond the child's original limited scope. This truth can often be lost on an employer who is so focused on her own vision that she ignores the scenery around her.

Alice: "Do you know, I always thought unicorns were fabulous monsters, too? I never saw one alive before!" Well, now that we have seen each other," said the unicorn, "if you'll believe in me, I'll believe in you. Is that a bargain?"

— Lewis Carroll, Alice's Adventures in Wonderland

The true impact of this is probably best expressed by my relationship with family and close-knit friends. I believe I know them and they know me. The safety zone that surrounds my home should be there to allow me to drop my guard, relax and feel safe. It also should be a space in which I can openly express my weakest moments. Those fears, disappointments and accomplishments won't risk my place in that 'home' or the spirit of belonging that exists. For many years, I avoided hiring anyone who wasn't related or previously connected to me in some way.

Annie's Honor Snacks was intended to be a family business from the beginning. When my father and uncle pulled out, I was forced to be on my own. My first husband occasionally contributed to the operations when he wasn't involved in another job. Fortunately, I secured employees who were self-motivated individuals. Since we had a pre-existing relationship, I felt reassured. Our mutual respect and appreciation for each other once nurtured, could grow. They understood clearly what had to be done and always followed through.

This, in part, could be attributed to the home environment and the casual and personal atmosphere in which we worked. I paid the wages but I also packed the snack boxes and made deliveries when I wasn't out securing new accounts. I led by example and active involvement.

My need for affirmation influenced my thought process and actions whenever I brought someone else into my business environment. I continued to be drawn to people I already knew whenever possible. With *AERIN, Inc.*, my husband's purchase of the additional customer-base, is a good example. It allowed a merger of our two businesses into a family partnership. We then shared common office space and staff. One prior employee from *Annie's Honor Snacks* joined us, extending the familiarity.

When I acquired a competitor's business, we hired my cousin's husband to join us. Talk about a major life-style change for him and his wife — They sold their home on Long Island, New York and moved to Vermont! Godmother to my daughter, my cousin and I have always been close and this allowed us to bond to an even greater degree. As couples, we enjoyed each other's company and spent many a weekend boating on Lake Champlain together.

Our new hire was high-energy, a team player, and great fun to be around. In some ways, he reminded me of Wonderland's 'Hatter'. Everyone couldn't help but love him for his spontaneous one-liners and gregarious personality that made him such a good salesperson.

At the time, I never realized how much I depended on him to fill that great divide that was secretly growing between my first husband and me. For three months, he lived with us while my cousin remained in New York to sell their home. After putting my daughter to bed for the night, he and I plotted and planned for hours about how to grow the business while my co-owner husband preferred watching television and drinking beer. This person also was a major supporter and promotor for Bookkeepers Professional Resources Association, (BKPR). Much of its success can be credited to his help.

When he elected to move on to other opportunities, I experienced a loss nearly as painful as my divorce. I felt devastated with a martyr-like mentality. We were reunited years later, when I rehired him to be my sales manager for *AERIN, Inc.* He joined George and me in our efforts to expand the business into New Hampshire. We welcomed him back with arms wide open.

I have allowed past judgements to be ruled by my fear of abandonment. Although that vulnerability goes back to certain childhood experiences, it has repeatedly played out in my business life. People come and go for reasons of their own that don't necessarily have anything to do with me personally. Their actions affect me by their leaving but they don't weaken me unless I allow them to do so. Disappointments and loss are equally as valuable as the surprises and good fortune life treats me.

To this day, I remember clearly how difficult the loss of an office manager had on me. Not only was she efficient at her job, but she was a joy to be around. Her energy and humor was infectious. It was so easy to get caught up in conversations with her and lose an hour of the day—and not regret one minute of it! She influenced who I hired and who I fired and her strong personality dominated the work environment and co-workers. When George and I looked to purchase a new home with additional space to accommodate an expanded home-office, she was a major influence in our decision because she required less than a 15-minute commute to work.

I tried to hang onto an atmosphere of familiarity I experienced with a smaller staff like *Annie's Honor Snacks*. I expected I could manage ten people the same way I managed two people. But with more staff, more personalities emerged, creating for me new challenges in standards, equality and performance.

There is always a boundary between employer and employee but I didn't want to realize the implications that can arise from that separateness. It wasn't wrong to get a valued employee's input nor even go along with her recommendations. What was misguided was my dependency on putting her choices ahead of my own. I would do just about anything I could afford to do to keep her on. I convinced myself that my business couldn't function without her.

But lose her, I did— Not once, but twice. It always began with a totally unexpected early morning phone call from her. It hurt deeply that she didn't tell me face-to-face and just announced her resignation on the phone with a standard two-week notice. I didn't understand that the relationship I envisioned we had wasn't the same for her. I had to accept the fact that ultimately, I wasn't more than the person writing her paycheck. Where her position was a job to her, to me I visualized it as a career. I should have told myself, "Buck-up, Annie! You are not the center of her universe."

Her first resignation was short-lived. The new job she had taken didn't live up to her expectations. I was over-joyed when she called and said she would come back to work for me. The second time she resigned, I was angry and upset. I felt betrayed. I couldn't stop myself from thinking, "I'm such a fool. Why did she not prepare me for this? Why didn't I see this coming?"

I was inconsolable and cried for days. For the next two weeks, until her keys were turned in and she left my employ permanently, I couldn't bring myself to go into the office for fear of having to face her. I concluded that somehow I must have messed up for her to leave. I wish I understood why she chose to end our relationship as she did.

About the same time, I was mired in the on-going recruiting for New Hampshire. My only child had moved more than nine hundred miles away. The recent new hire in the Vermont office was barely trained and not ready to take on the full responsibilities of her new position. We had just moved to a new home and Christmas was only days away.

The mindset I was in was not healthy. After I got over myself, I concluded that 'Blame' only prolongs grief. 'Regret,' I could deal with. At least, it leaves the door cracked open for 'Change' to make its way through.

I have always chosen to associate with other people to make my world complete. And yet, I cannot presume that their choice to let me share in their lives will match my standards of what I want the relationship to be. I can no more dictate their path than they can define mine. The best I can do is be present in the time we are together and listen with an open mind. My character is my defining quality.

Honest communication is key. It doesn't exist if I only hear myself speak and don't make a point to find out if I am truly being understood. The so-called betrayal I have felt is compounded by my own inefficiencies.

In retrospect, I think I was most inclined to hire family because I was afraid. I didn't know how to hire the right person and thought by doing this I was lessening my chances of hiring the wrong person for the job. A stranger might take advantage, see through a crack in my armor and recognize just how vulnerable and unsure of myself I often could be.

Through *my* eyes, family had already passed judgement, knew my weaknesses, so I had nothing to prove. My ex-husband once told me, that I should just try to be the face of the business, and he would provide the brains. I could be a bit player, a great fill-in, but never actually the star. For many years, I bought into that role. He controlled the books and I dealt with HR and customer and community relations.

How foolish! I trapped myself into believing that what I perceived others thought of me, defined my quality as a person-- even though, I really didn't know what others thought-- because I never took the chance to ask. Why would I put so much significance on what others thought? It always came down to what I thought of myself. Now doesn't that sound just like the crazy nonsense that existed in Wonderland?

> *"Always speak the truth, think before you speak, and write it down afterwards."*
>
> — *Lewis Carroll, Alice's Adventures in Wonderland*

For a short time, I hired my daughter to work for me in New Hampshire when she was fresh out of college. Her newly developed talents and youthful appeal encouraged me to expand my business services to include logo and graphic design work. I also purchased an industrial strength embroidery machine and software to accommodate customers needing small quantity orders of branded apparel.

This was a relatively new product line for us. I argued that most of my small business customers didn't have a need for large quantities of silkscreened and embroidered products. It didn't take long to realize that the process for embroidering garments required a significant amount of time and skill, making those small quantities cost prohibitive. Now I understood why other companies were requiring the higher minimum orders.

Companies that specialized in garment decorations typically had more machinery in their shop. For larger orders, our single head embroidery machine was only capable of stitching one garment at a time. It became a grueling process that required someone to tend the machine constantly when in production.

It also didn't occur to me that perhaps this product line appealed to a different market segment. Even with the adequate training we received, there was a significant learning curve. I had to not only learn and train my people to become fluent in the finer points of this industry, but I had to reassess what customers to target and focus my efforts building those relationships.

Direct sales proved not to be my daughter's calling. Moreover, she took the job out of a need for employment with a guaranteed income, a nice place to live, and a way to help her Mom. I was so caught up with my vision that I overlooked just how much experience, training and consistent leadership was necessary to ensure her success. It was doubly hard since her only support was coming from me her mother, or else her cousin (my Sales Manager), and we were three hours driving time away.

She took the job for the wrong reasons, but I was guilty of a far more serious crime. As much as I wanted to help her get a good start in life-after-college, I was feeding my need to keep my daughter near to me and be a valued part of her world.

Less than a year later, my daughter packed her car with as much of her belongings that could fit and headed south to start a new life and begin a new career for herself. It was time for her to venture down a path of her choosing and it was time for me to let her go.   My daughter will always be my most cherished gift this world has bestowed on me. I am so proud of her strength and her determination to overcome obstacles big and small. Smart, creative and playful (when she lets herself be), she is often my source of inspiration.

It was a difficult decision for me to hire my husband George to work for my business. I was indecisive because I feared I would jeopardize our personal relationship. I tortured myself with second-guessing. Was part of the reason my first marriage ended because my husband and I worked together? I knew that for George to work with me, he must work *for* me and that isn't an easy feat, especially with both of us under the same roof, 24/7.

When I first met George he was transitioning from a property manager position into a self-employed free-lance bookkeeper. *(The story of how we met is the basis for yet another book).* Fourteen years my senior and retired 20-year Air Force veteran, this man is my favorite companion and confidante. Both of us are flawed. Both of us have our weaknesses. At times, we have hurt each other so deeply, that it would have justifiably led other couples to divorce.

We have discovered that somewhere along our journey we have committed ourselves to each other's happiness and peace. I pledged to trust this man with my life; and in so doing, he should expect nothing less from me.   As our relationship has developed and matured over the years, he has remained by my side through all the turmoil life has thrown our way.

George has never felt intimidated or less of a person because I am the boss of my business. We have our moments, but he always appears by my side when I need him the most, helping me in any way he can. Every day I am thankful for that. He is my Cheshire Cat, and occasionally appears and disappears at will especially when I'm "strictly all business." He can baffle and annoy me with his random philosophical points and quirky stream-of-consciousness thoughts, but his positive view of life, that grin of his, stays with me long after the rest fades away.

Just placing the entrepreneurial crown on my head doesn't mean I am in command of my business. I cannot do my queenly duties well without the aid of the other characters in my court. Hiring family won't guarantee success. It is my leadership skills and perceptions that will make my reign memorable. If I inspire others to realize *my* dream, I can create a team that is self-motivated, happy and dedicated to serving our customers and supporting each other. My enterprise becomes so much more. It is a business with a soul.

"Every story has a moral you just need to be clever enough to find it." (the Duchess)

— Lewis Carroll, *Though the Looking Glass*

WHƏT EyES SEE

Everyone has stories to share. Funny, sad, inspiring and tragic— whatever the case may be, my stories provide the emotional attraction I use to give me reign over my entrepreneurial realm. The other characters that reside with me or those who happen to visit, make my 'Queendom' real-- even when I consistently am recreating my own reality. Whenever I deviate from the script, everyone connected to me and my business will feel some degree of the after-effects.

Most experienced business professionals realize that marketing encompasses only the mediums through which we identify and communicate what our business offers; whereas, branding embraces everything that represents the business's intentions and ethics. I love that branding is fundamental. It is basic and it's got to have soul. My brand, my sense of self as well as my sense of business, is dependent upon taking advantage of my most meaningful memories. Without memory to remind me of who I am, I have no identity. My unique brand becomes invisible.

"I wonder if I've been changed in the night? Let me think.
Was I the same when I got up this morning?
I almost think I can remember feeling a little different.
But if I'm not the same, the next question is 'Who in the
world am I?' Ah, that's the great puzzle!" (Alice)

— Lewis Carroll, Alice's Adventures In Wonderland

Annie's Honor Snacks provides a good example of this. When I started that business, I was coming from a teaching background. It was natural for me to use the familiar recognition of student achievement that schools use as part of my brand imaging. Companies who signed up for my service gave me their business card to add to my "Honor Roll" credits.

This was a great marketing tool for approaching new prospects and building my credibility. They would be able to see page after page of business cards I collected -- the cards of their competitors' and other business names they recognized-- all using my service. Of course, they wanted to be on the 'Honor Roll' too!

My honor-snack boxes always served fresh, individually priced and wrapped snacks and gourmet baked goods. The added "wow" was that the contents were customized to each location based on their choice of treats that they selected from an extensive menu. *Annie's Honor Snacks* was not made for big business or corporations. This customization appealed to a select group of small business owners reinforcing my brand's message about uniqueness and service.

Each box featured my logoed gold seal, complete with a halo. They came in 3 different sizes, made of royal blue-colored corrugated plastic (for easy cleaning) with built-in handles. Once filled with the snacks and the coin container, the snack boxes' plaid "picnic bonnet" stretched over its top, sheltering the goods inside. With the right presentation and packaging, my snack boxes filled a need that a vending machine could not meet and conveyed a brand that spoke of honesty, trust, simplicity and "home-made" appeal. Sometimes people can over-complicate the process for developing their unique brand. I recommend entrepreneurs to use their hobbies and interests as potential resources for finding that special distinctive characteristic that hooks the target audience. It is fun and surprising the number of wonderful ideas that can be used. Branding provides a great opportunity to let individual talents and skills thrive outside of what would be considered the norm for a traditional work-place.

Most importantly, engaging in activities that utilize my unique personal brand does not constitute a huge financial investment. My Bachelor of Arts degree was in Theatre Arts and my teaching certification was in Communications. On the surface, those achievements would hardly seem significant to running a business. Yet, I have been able to consistently tap into that knowledge and experience over the years. Here are a few examples:

Teaching skills:
- Training employees, facilitating workshops,
- Leading discussion groups

Theatre Arts:

- Creative marketing ideas for myself and advising others

- Creating uniquely different trade show displays (Note: *AERIN, Inc.* was awarded "The Best in Show" for 5 consecutive years at the Vermont Business and Industry Expo)

- At ease speaking in front of small or large audiences

- Organizing and promoting business events and trade shows for customers

Self-made, experienced entrepreneur:

- Knowing the difference between working on my business and working in my business

- Able to provide the benefits that result from being a trusted advisor

- First-hand experience being a business owner

Branding should be taken seriously as an amalgamation of consistently portrayed characteristics that include products and services, personality, quality, reputation, and origin— to name a few. It is unfortunate when small companies and startups confuse a logo and tagline as their branding solution, settling on just the visual image of who they are. It is far from the truth.

A business should focus on generating an emotional response, consistently reinforcing that same experience and communicating it to an ever-expanding audience. The goal is to have people recognize it without detailed explanations. When we see an apple symbol with a chunk bitten out of it, we know it is Apple Computer™. When we see a swish on the side of an athletic shoe, we know it is Nike™. Michael Eisner, former Chief Executive Officer of The Walt Disney Company once said, "A brand is a living entity—and it is enriched or undermined cumulatively over time, the product of a thousand small gestures."

Back in 2008, the recession significantly impacted *AERIN, Inc.* as well as the exploding use of the internet. I was fortunate to have the recognition and reputation of the *Safeguard™* brand behind me. Some of the factors that impacted my business directly, included:

- Some of our customers, to conserve spending, reduced their inventory of print products, or avoided ordering all together. Price shopping for some became a necessity even if they sacrificed our higher standards of quality and service.

- There were businesses that closed their doors rather than try to compete against the emerging internet service providers and the rapid advancements in technology that were negatively impacting their business.

- ROI decreased.

Several years earlier, anticipating the decline in computer checks and forms as offices strove to become 'paperless,' we began to shift our focus to promotional products in addition to logoed corporate apparel. Marketing would soon become our primary catalyst for business growth. The recession slowed our progress in introducing this new product line. It also gave us time to ramp-up and obtain the information and training we needed to become experts in the field. Where our brand had been previously focused on business management products and services, we were now challenged to re-brand ourselves as a viable resource for commercial print and marketing solutions.

I have learned that entrepreneurs must always be ready for change. Their businesses, like their business plans must be fluid and adaptable to flow with such things as a changing economy, unforeseen setbacks and growth spurts. When times are lean, sometimes businesses make the mistake of cutting back on their marketing efforts. When asked, I am often told that they rely on "word of mouth" to grow their business. They often turn to do-it-yourself solutions for marketing pieces such as business cards and flyers with only cost in mind, never realizing they are diluting their uniqueness and brand image or overlooking it all together.

This can be a huge mistake. Those first impressions are lasting impressions. It's quite basic, really. Unless a business is consistently having a positive marketing presence it will not grow.

A business without a minimum of modest growth in its customer base to offset attrition will eventually cease to exist. It is at the most difficult of times when a well-planned and executed marketing strategy is the most crucial for an entrepreneur. Plan a long-term strategy. Execute it wisely. Monitor and measure its results.

By 2010, I had come to admit that I needed to reassess my business and my life. I was no longer content just selling products or services. George and I were stressed and discouraged as we were still trying to increase sales in New Hampshire.

We knew that something needed fixing but couldn't quite see how our current situation could adapt to the dramatic changes we envisioned. We believed that to remain competitive in the marketplace we had to offer a uniqueness that would distinguish us from other people in our increasingly competitive industry. I wanted to reinvent my image from a sales person to a knowledgeable business advisor.

> *"You're not the same as you were before," he said.*
> *You were much more... muchier... you've lost your*
> *muchness."*
>
> —*Lewis Carroll, Alice's Adventures in Wonderland*

I already had years of training and experience under my belt. I was an experienced teacher and presenter. I had spent seven years under the tutelage of a practiced and highly respected business and life coach. I had lived the life as an entrepreneur and woman business owner in a male-dominated professional world. It was time to put my talents and know-how to good use.

I sold my existing base of business to a trusted colleague who I had come to know over the years and who shared my experiences as a *Safeguard Business Systems™* distributor. He has an ambitious and progressive enterprise spanning several states. His buying my business allowed George and me to begin anew with our life purpose driving our actions for creating a legacy of leadership and value to small business owners.

We wanted to settle in a warmer climate with our eyes on retirement over the horizon. We also were looking for a robust business community with a diverse and growing population that supported entrepreneurs. We chose South Carolina, eventually ending up in a town conveniently close to the border of Charlotte, North Carolina. And so, a new life-journey began.

We knew no one in the area, nor had an existing customer base to utilize. For the first time, I experienced urban traffic. (I'm not sure I will ever get comfortable with city driving). Staving-off panic, we put together a simple game plan:

> *Step 1:* Make new friends
> *Step 2:* Promote our brand recognition as an authority in our field.
> *Step 3:* Develop a market that will provide us with the least resistance and shortest sales cycle.
> *Step 4:* Convert that new market into a solid customer base and utilize it as referral sources to obtain qualified prospects.
> *Step 5:* Get involved in business community activities and events

Our first step and logical choice was joining the local Chamber of Commerce and actively participating in its events and programs. We attended other business networking meetings as well. Mastermind groups, referral groups, lead generation groups, self-help groups, network marketing groups... Ah, there were so many groups!

There are so many professional organizations where I live that I could literally attend meetings from early morning to late at night, every day of the week. I have met individuals who have based their careers on attending networking functions. I watch others follow them from one event to another just like Alice follows the White Rabbit. Secretly I wonder if their professional endeavors are as successful as they lead others to believe. Did I see a look of self-doubt cross her face? Isn't he representing a different company, his third career change in less than a year?

Networking events do provide movement, motivation, brand exposure and the delightful human contact we need to experience as part of a larger community. After all, it makes us feel good. We are getting out of the house. We are presenting our business and building our brand through repetition. However, this becomes senseless activity without a concentrated thought process for the desired outcome. Many entrepreneurs chose this path because they justify it as a relatively modest expense to promote their business compared to other promotional efforts.

I tried leadership roles in such groups serving on the board of directors, acting as meeting facilitator and participating as chapter officer. At one point, I formed an LLC with two other partners and launched our own collaborative of business service providers. The time-consuming demands in building, managing and leading such an organization quickly outweighed my original reason for my involvement in the first place: to grow my business. I didn't set out to begin a new business, it just morphed into one.

My intention was to take the business I had and bring it to another level of achievement. I got side-tracked and nearly lost my way—again. With practice I've become more selective as to which networking groups I wish to join. Allowing myself to become actively involved, I track the impact each membership has on my business and carefully compare it to the cost of my time and other related expenses.

The quality of the group is critical. I look for those that provide activities or speakers who have knowledge to share that will increase my personal or professional development. I do not attend any of these meetings with a notion that a sale will ultimately take place. I look instead for substance and direction, not just a place to give my 30 second spiel of who I am and pass out a bunch of business cards.

It is usually that time before and after the meeting where serious opportunities to connect with someone occurs. That is when I can pre-qualify a person as someone who I can potentially collaborate with, who might require my services, or provide me the opportunity to guide someone I know to them. Scheduling a one-on-one appointment follows.

I know the freedom and ability to express my brand in all that I do allows me to experience a symmetry that leaves me fulfilled. This 'place' is where my business and my life can truly serve each other. I do not need to be a different person at work and another one at home— one 'me' will suffice, thank you. I validate my commitments to my career and my devotion and responsibilities to my family and myself, not as sacrifices or obligations but as conscious choices. My brand has purpose. All I must do is continue to communicate it to others with consistency.

I find great pleasure in helping businesses uncover their unique brand and understand its relevance. There is a desire within me to educate, train and provide business owners with ideas and strategies to help them effectively maximize their brand identifiers. When I can consult with the business owner or evolving entrepreneur to understand the underlying principles that motivates them, I can help them focus on their true purpose for being an entrepreneur. That purpose becomes the foundation to any recommendations I make.

I am a 'Brandologist.' I specialize in the art of branding. I am devoted to providing meaningful and valued advice to businesses establishing their presence in the world of their choosing.

ALL GROWN UP

"But then, shall I never get any older than
  I am now?
That will be a comfort, one way —
never to be an old woman —
But then — always to have lessons to learn!" (Alice)

— Lewis Carroll, *Alice's Adventures in Wonderland*

As I've matured in age and experience, I spend more time refining who I am and what I do and less time taking on brand new enterprises. My changes require much subtler shifts in my mindset yet they still excite me in ways that keep me looking for new adventures and possibilities.

This is the last chapter of this book– but certainly not the conclusion of my entrepreneurial quest for this lifetime. I hope I have portrayed some examples to the blossoming entrepreneur that fear is real but not an insurmountable barrier on the road to success. As these are my confessions as an entrepreneur, I must fess-up and admit I am still evolving. All grown up? Hardly! Why, there's just no fun in that. Following is a summation of what I've shared.

Choosing the life of an entrepreneur is not a substitute for an unhappy job situation. It doesn't guarantee shorter work days or bigger pay checks. What it does provide is the personal freedom to pursue ideas and ventures by choice when enhanced with a well defined purpose. The entrepreneur will embrace change and remember it is what drove him down the self-employment path in the first place.

A successful entrepreneur perseveres despite the business challenges that are encountered with large doses of patience and commitment. The end goal must always remain clear and realistic while accommodating necessary changes that are bound to happen unexpectedly. When certain practices are utilized in a business, they will ensure a lasting stability no matter the structure, size or complexity of the enterprise. They include an understanding of financial management and legal responsibilities, defined management standards and systems to implement processes and functionality and strategic marketing practices to leverage brand identity and recognition.

Part of being an entrepreneur is taking risks— with those risks, one is bound to experience failure at some point in time. It is all a part of the process of development through adaptability. It is natural to feel frustrated when trying something new doesn't go according to plan. That is the time when trusting and believing in one's dream will make the journey worth while. The important message is to never give up.

People are influenced by many things. One's personal upbringing and life experiences will always influence the decision-making processes because they are a segment of who we are. Realizing that they exist provide opportunities to break-out of the confines we have allowed to imprison us and convert them into personal strengths and attributes we can put to better use.

The entrepreneur who is convinced that going it alone is

limiting both business and personal development. Impartial advisors can reduce costly mistakes and wasted time. Most importantly, they can contribute a different perspective that may never have been considered. Don't try to know everything. Know your strengths and seek out others who will be committed to providing the skills and talents you find lacking.

Leadership is a learned trait. It is not a genetic characteristic. A good leader encourages others to succeed by reinforcing their accomplishments through recognition and rewards. Consistently live the vision of your enterprise by inspiring and guiding employees and customers through example. Seek out the company of others whom you admire and can learn from. Leaders can be found in every walk of life and are recognized by their pursuit of knowledge, humility and generosity to others.

Communicate a compelling brand and tell a unique story to attract prospects and connect with customers. Define that brand identifier that best represents you and your ability to provide the necessities that your customers will use and need. With an extensive marketing and promotional plan, incorporate creative and diverse strategies that are purposeful and can be measured for their effectiveness.

Now grab your laptop, tablet or notepad. Begin writing down what it means to be an entrepreneur-- just for you. What do you visualize for your entrepreneurial destiny? Capture it in your memories so you don't forget.

Are you ready to make a promise to yourself?

Go for it.

NOTES

All quotes are credited directly from Lewis Carroll's
Alice's Adventures in Wonderland (1865) and Through the
Looking Glass and What Alice Found There (1871). Both
Alice books were copyright protected until 42 years after
the first publication or seven years after the author's death,
whichever was the longer. There was a 1911 Act that
replaced the 1842 Copyright Act, extending the period to
50 years after Carroll's death. The copyright on Alice's
Adventures in Wonderland subsisted until 1907 and that of
Through the Looking-Glass and What Alice Found There
until 1948.

1. From Wikipedia, the free encyclopedia (GNU Free
   Documentation License), Permanent link:
   https://en.wikipedia.org/w/index.php?
   title=GNU_Free_Documentation_License&oldid=7742
   37249):

   a. **Stage**: The first public stage adaptation of
      "Alice's Adventures in Wonderland", "Alice in
      Wonderland", debuted at the Royal Polytechnic
      Institute in London, England, on 17 April 1876.
      The musical, "Alice in Wonderland, a Dream
      Play for Children," was performed 23 December
      1886 at the Prince of Wales Theatre in London,
      and continued until 18 March 1887. It was later
      revived and performed at the Globe Theatre
      from 26 December 1888 to 9 February 1889.

Frequently revived during the "Christmas season", it was produced eighteen times from 1898 to 1930. "Alice's Adventures in Wonderland" has since been adapted for various forms of the stage, including ballets, operas, experimental theatre, Broadway musicals, puppet plays, mime acts, and rock musicals.

b. **Film and television:** Debuted in Great Britain in 1903 as a silent film and in January 1904 in the United States. Two more silent film adaptations of "Alice's Adventures in Wonderland" were produced: one in 1910 and another in 1915. The first Alice film with sound (1931). Other adaptations were released in 1933, 1948, and Kathryn Beaumont voiced her in the Walt Disney's film of 1951. Alice has also been portrayed by Fiona Fullerton (1972), Amelia Shankley and Coral Browne (1985), Kristyna Kohoutova (1988), and Mia Wasikowska, who notably played Alice as a teenager as opposed to a child in the 2010 release. Actors who portrayed or voiced Alice in television-film adaptations include Janet Waldo (1966), Anne-Marie Malik (1966), Natalie Gregory (1985), and Tina Majorino (1999).

a. *"Alice in Wonderland"* is a 1951 British-American animated fantasy comedy-adventure film produced by Walt Disney Productions and based primarily on Lewis Carroll's Alice's Adventures in Wonderland with several additional elements from his sequel, Through the Looking-Glass. The 13th Disney animated feature film, it was released in New York City and London on July 26, 1951, and features the voices of Kathryn Beaumont as Alice, and Ed Wynn as the Mad Hatter. The theme song, "Alice in Wonderland", has since become a jazz standard.

b. *"Alice in Wonderland"* was produced (live-action) as a 2010 American fantasy film directed by Tim Burton and written by Linda Woolverton. Released by Walt Disney Pictures, the film stars Mia Wasikowska, Johnny Depp, AnneHathaway and Helena Bonhm Carter. The film was shot in the United Kingdom and the United States.

c. *"Alice Through the Looking Glass"* is a 2016 American fantasy film directed by James Bobin film stars Mia Wasikowska, Johnny Depp, Helena Bonham Carter, Anne Hathaway, Sacha Baron Cohen, and Rhys Ifans, and was released on May 27, 2016.

Illustrations and Book Cover

Matt Vasey is an artist, designer and illustrator from Pennsylvania. A Lock Haven University graduate with a Bachelor of Arts in Fine Art, he loves drawing in various mediums. Matt has been employed by Safeguard for the past 20 years and has held a number of printing and manufacturing positions. His current post is in Safeguard's Design Services department.

Preface

1. Wikipedia, last edited May 3, 2017. Creative Commons Attribution-Shouldlike. Wikimedia Foundation, Inc. External links: Ghandi, Laksmi (Aug. 26, 2013), "A History of Snake Oil Salesmen," National Public Radio, CodeSwitch@nprcodeswitch.com

Chapter 1

1. Covey, Stephen H., The 8th Habit, New York, Free Press, (2004).

2. *Father Knows Best*, Television series (1954-1960), Rodney/ Young Production, a Screen Gems Production, copyright (1954-1963).

3. *Leave It to Beaver*, Television series (1957-1963), Gomalco Productions, Kayro-Vue Productions, Original network CBS (1957-1958), ABC (1958-1963).

4. *I Love Lucy*, CBS television series (1951-1957), and seceded by several special episodes and series variations such as *The Lucy Show* (1962-1968) and *Here's Lucy* (1968-1974). Original producers: Jeff Oppenheimer and Desi Arnaz.

5. *Honeymooners*, CBS television series sitcom (1951-1955). Originated from the DuMont the network's variety show, *The Jackie Gleason Show* which was broadcast live before a studio audience. Producers: Jack Philbin, Stanley Poss, Jackie Gleason Enterprises.

6. *The Mary Tyler Moore Show*, CBS television series sitcom created by James L. Brooks and Allan Burns, (1970-1977), MTM Enterprises.

7. Bradberry, Travis and Greaves, Jean, <u>Emotional Intelligence 2.0</u>, TalentSmart, (2009) page 20.

8. Woodward, Orrin and Brady, Chris, <u>Financial Fitness</u>, Obstaclés Press, by Life Leadership, (2014) page 182.

9. www.goodreads.com, Goodreads, Inc., Silverstein, Shel, (2002), <u>Where the Sidewalk Ends</u>, HarperCollins Children's Books, (first published 1974).

Chapter 2

1. Gerber, Michael E., <u>The E-Myth Revisited</u>, New York, Harper Business, HarperCollins Publishers, (1995). Chapter 9.

Chapter 3

1. Colby, Sandra L. and Ortman, Jennifer M., "The Baby Boom Cohort in the United States: 2012-2060," Current Population Reports, P25-1141. U.S. Census Bureau, Washington, DC), 2014.

2. Loring, Devin, "Why Is the Wellness Industry Booming? Ask Boomers," Ashbury Park Press, Part of the USA Today Network, (September 5, 2015).

3. Stack, Jack, The Great Game of Business, Currency and Doubleday, (1994) p.175.

4. Burrows, Jeff, Thought Leader, Author, Speaker, Business/Life Coach.(www.jeffburrows.com).

5. Johansson, Anna, "The 7 Biggest Challenges That Small Business Owners Face in 2016," Inc. Magazine, (April 21, 2016) cover story.

6. "Mini-Me." Collins English Dictionary – Complete and Unabridged, 12th Edition 2014. 1991, 1994, 1998, 2000, 2003, 2006, 2007, 2009, 2011, 2014. HarperCollins Publishers 20 May. 2017 http://www.thefreedictionary.com/Mini-Me

Chapter 4

1. Gardner, Jennifer M. (1994). "The 1990-1991 Recession: How Bad was the Labor Market?" (PDF). *Monthly Labor Review*. Bureau of Labor Statistics. **117** (6): 3–11. Retrieved 6 April 2011.

Chapter 6

1. U.S. Small Business Administration, Official web site: sba.gov, (Home page), published April, 2017. Produced in partnership with the U.S. Small Business Administration, Business Gateway and ENERGY STAR®

2. Gran, Ben, "Shocking U.S. Home Based Business Statistics," (incfile.com), March 21, 2017. - See more at: https://www.incfile.com/blog/post/shocking-us-home-based-business-statistics/#sthash.MRm0TOZB.dpuf

Chapter 7

1. The American Institute of Stress, a Texas 501(3)c nonprofit corporation, article: "Workplace Stress," appeared on web site, Stress.org, Copyright 1979-2017.

2. Gerber, Michael E., The E-Myth Revisited, New York, Harper Business, HarperCollins Publishers, (1995).